AN ATHLETE'S
PERSPECTIVE

AN ATHLETE'S PERSPECTIVE

——A Guide to Success——

Dealing with Success, Failure, Expectation, Pressure Practice, and the Mental Game

INCLUDES TWO PERSONAL STORIES FROM ATHLETES
BY RUTHIE BOLTON, A TWO-TIME OLYMPIC GOLD MEDALIST,
and RICHARD BATTLES—"Journey to a Half-Tri Event"

Written from my heart to provide knowledge, information, and hope to
anyone who wants to reach their full potential at any endeavor

S. J. BATTLES
A PROFESSIONAL ATHLETE

Order this book online at www.trafford.com
or email orders@trafford.com

Most Trafford titles are also available at major online book retailers.

Printed in the United States of America.

ISBN: 978-1-4669-7367-1 (sc)
ISBN: 978-1-4669-7368-8 (e)

Library of Congress Control Number: 2012923925

Trafford rev. 01/17/2013

www.trafford.com

North America & international
toll-free: 1 888 232 4444 (USA & Canada)
phone: 250 383 6864 ♦ fax: 812 355 4082

CONTENTS

PREFACE.. 1

IN A NUTSHELL.. 5

INTRODUCTION 9

PHYSICAL PRACTICE.. 11

MENTAL PRACTICES.. 30

EXPECTATION AND PRESSURE................................ 43

SUCCESS AND FAILURE.. 48

KEYS FOR REACHING YOUR HIGHEST POTENTIAL...................... 55

EXPANSION OF KEYS.. 64

STORIES FROM ATHLETES...................................... 76

CONCLUSION.. 93

HIGHLY RECOMMENDED BOOKS AND MOVIES 95

ACKNOWLEDGMENTS 97

Dedicated to Larry Mathews.
God rest his soul.

Larry taught me much of the information provided for you. It is important that his knowledge is passed on. Larry was my best teacher and one of my very best friends. He made me a "player", a champion and most importantly a much better person. He also saved my life in many ways.

I will always love you, Larry.

IF YOU FAIL TO PLAN, YOU PLAN TO FAIL.

CONFIDENCE IS KNOWING YOU ARE PREPARED.

KNOWLEDGE EQUALS NO FEAR.

ALWAYS

ENJOY YOUR JOURNEY . . .

PREFACE

It has been very exciting for me to get so many things I have learned throughout my sports journey down on paper. The first draft was 138 pages, and now, there are two short books about 45 pages each. The titles are A GUIDE TO SUCCESS and YOUTH COACHING/SPORTS MENTORING.

I must share a few personal things with you before you begin reading this information. Please keep in mind that I am just an ordinary person who went to school and then a job and achieved success at work and outside of work based on all the information I am presenting to you.

I had very low points and many negative experiences in my life, especially during my childhood. I lived in a dysfunctional situation and was heavily criticized for my features and being competitive. During my twenties, I became determined to have a happy adulthood and prove to myself that I was not what "they" said I was. I carried a lot of anger and pain. I was fortunate to follow a positive path. I was able to take my anger and pain and focus that energy into sports and hard work. I know because I kept doing what I loved, competing, that it saved my life. I loved to compete. I played softball, volleyball, basketball, soccer, tetherball, and marbles. I roller-skated, skateboarded, and played chess.

At twenty-six, I focused on one sport and became a professional bowler by age thirty at the regional level, and I was successful. Bowling was a fifteen-year journey of my life, and it is the sport that really taught me most of what I am presenting to you about how to reach your highest potential. I also learned a huge amount from my bowling teacher, Larry Mathews. Since retiring from bowling at age forty and my thirty-three-year PG&E career at age fifty-five, I have coached girls' basketball, mentored youth, and played golf for personal enjoyment.

I really just want it to be clear to you that I have used and lived everything I have written in this book, and I believe it can all work for anyone. Even parts of it can work. I want to share what I learned to help our youth or anyone not to give up and to pursue success at what they love. Setting goals, working hard, and achieving goals will bring a lot of satisfaction, peace of mind, and happiness. This information is what I learned during my personal life and sport journeys.

I believe extracurricular activities are a lot of what keeps us all going. Youth involved in anything positive is good. By learning how to become successful at what you love to do, it will help you to stick with all your goals. Never give up on positive activities. Stay involved with good groups.

I strongly believe every person should find something that they love and give their very best to reach their highest potential at it. In turn, this creates a valuable life-learning experience. Working hard at something you love will help you learn how to deal with many things that life can throw your way. If every child and adult stayed involved with a positive group, the whole world would be a better place.

In order to reach your highest potential, you must become dedicated to what you love, learn to schedule your time, work hard, and never give up on yourself. Do not let anyone discourage you. Do not buy into negative statements made to you. You must believe in yourself and pursue your own dreams. Achieving your goals and living your dreams are up to you.

I have not read too much of the Bible, but I did run across something from the book of Corinthians that really touched me. When I read it, it made me think about how I feel about teaching and especially teaching our youth. When you read the verse, it should help you to understand that I wrote all this down out of love. I want to share this knowledge with you because it made my life so much better. I want it to help your journey be more positive.

IF I SPEAK IN THE TONGUES OF MEN AND OF ANGELS

BUT HAVE NOT LOVE

I AM A NOISY GONG OR A CLANGING CYMBAL
AND IF I HAVE PROPHETIC POWERS, AND UNDERSTAND ALL
MYSTERIES AND ALL KNOWLEDGE, AND IF I HAVE ALL FAITH, SO AS
TO REMOVE MOUNTAINS,

BUT HAVE NOT LOVE

I AM NOTHING

IF I GIVE AWAY ALL I HAVE, AND IF I DELIVER MY BODY TO BE
BURNED

BUT HAVE NOT LOVE
I GAIN NOTHING

LOVE IS PATIENT AND KIND
LOVE IS NOT JEALOUS OR BOASTFUL
IT IS NOT ARROGANT OR RUDE
LOVE DOES NOT INSIST ON ITS OWN WAY
IT IS NOT IRRITABLE OR RESENTFUL
IT DOES NOT REJOICE AT WRONG, BUT REJOICES IN THE RIGHT

LOVE BEARS ALL THINGS

BELIEVES ALL THINGS, HOPES ALL THINGS,

ENDURES ALL THINGS,

LOVE NEVER ENDS.

(1 CORINTHIANS 13:1-8)

3

No one becomes successful without help and support. Seek good teachers and mentors and listen to their advice. Take notes, pay attention, and keep making good choices for you. Most importantly, I hope you enjoy this, learn new information, and learn to understand how to ALWAYS ENJOY YOUR JOURNEY.

IN A NUTSHELL

You choose your endeavor, travel through your journey,
and reach your highest potential.

The GOAL is to MASTER your endeavor physically and mentally while you
ENJOY YOUR JOURNEY. IF IT WAS EASY,
EVERYBODY WOULD BE DOING IT.

Traveling through your journey is where all the physical and mental challenges are. The goal is for you to travel through your journey with mental confidence. What it is really all about is ENJOYING YOUR JOURNEY.

This is especially written for athletes, competitors, and students involved in any endeavor. You will learn about the importance of dealing with failure, success, expectation, and pressure. Patience, discipline, self-responsibility, practice methods, and appropriate mental thought during practice and competition will be thoroughly covered. These methods can work for anyone working to achieve goals, regardless of your mental, physical, or athletic situation.

Most athletes have very strong egos. Some let their ego stop them from learning. Competitors at all levels can use this knowledge. Many athletes believe that hard work and practice are all that it takes to reach the high levels of competition. This information will help you to learn that there is more to it than that. Practice and hard work are only part of the formula.

Why is a poker player successful? They just sit there and play. Is it just luck? Once you begin to break into the top 10%, a lot of what happens depends upon what is in your mind. How you handle failure, success, pressure, and expectation become very critical. Once you reach the top 1% or 2% groups, what is in your mind becomes a very large percentage of determining your success. These groups are high-level teams or individuals of any age and the professional level.

Think about it: everyone around you has all the ability and skills to perform. What is it that creates that very special athlete, the athlete that seems to have everything go their way? It is true that high-level athletes are gifted with athletic ability. It is that ability, hard work, and practice that will get an athlete into the top 10%. At this level, it is time to have your mind in the right place to continue your journey to the very top.

The sooner an athlete learns the information in this book, the better. The elite athletes began learning much of this information at a very young age. Most were fortunate enough to have the talent and the proper guidance. There are a lot of big-time athletes who fail for various reasons, such as drugs, crime, or simply giving up. They did not have the proper guidance all along or did not listen to it.

This is all about learning how to get out of your own way in order to become successful at what you love doing, staying on the correct path, and ENJOYING YOUR JOURNEY. These ideas and theories will be a big assist for the athlete to reach their highest potential.

WHAT HAVE YOU GOT TO LOSE?
READ. YOU MIGHT JUST LEARN SOMETHING.

There is nothing like real-life experiences. Real-life experiences make a large impact, and experience cannot be taught or bought. An athlete can't know what great failure and success feel like until they are experienced. The important part is how those experiences, feelings, and what goes on in your mind are dealt with. How the athlete deals with the ups and downs of competition is what is critical.

This information will give you theories on how the mental and physical work together. Don't ever forget that all successful people did not become successful on their own. Seek and find good teachers; use your positive resources. Teachers, guides, parents, and mentors are very important parts of an athlete's success. Reading and learning the information here will help the athlete to KNOW when they have found a true teacher.

The goal here is to help athletes become less frustrated and get much more enjoyment out of what they are doing. There is more than meets the eye to getting this situation to occur. By learning and using these principles and ideas, your journey as an athlete should become a more positive experience from the lower levels through the top levels. We should always be

ENJOYING

OUR

JOURNEY.

INTRODUCTION

Why aren't you CONFIDENT? Have you ever been asked that question? You should be more CONFIDENT. Has that been said to you? Then you ask yourself, "How do I get CONFIDENCE?" Has anyone been able to answer that question for you? Do people see the ability, drive, desire, and heart and also see that you are not CONFIDENT? It would be great to feel truly confident, wouldn't it? You need a true teacher, but they are hard to find. As you read ahead, you will learn how to be a mentally and physically confident athlete.

A good teacher can improve your physical ability to its maximum. That is only 10% of the battle. The other 90% is the MENTAL part of competition. When you reach high levels of competition, the game becomes about 90% mental. Everyone at the top has the physical abilities to be a professional. It is the mental part that makes the difference in being successful. In an individual sport, you will stick out like a sore thumb if you do not have your head in the right place and a good, solid mental game. In a team sport, you may not stick out as much, but you may be the one who fails in the face of pressure. In most cases, the most accomplished athletes have great mental games. Many great athletes cannot put into words why they are successful. As an athlete, your successes and failures have about 90% to do with the mental knowledge and mental attitude that you possess.

There is a process to learning the mental game, and it works. Open your mind and heart to learning more. This information will help you reach your highest potential.

You may believe you are a winner, but at times, you feel like a loser. Once you learn to combine knowledge with hard work, you will know you are a winner. Become a complete player physically and, most importantly, mentally. The transition to the top of your game will be incredible. The journey during your transformation is what it is all about. Learn more about yourself, gain confidence and mental knowledge of your sport. Failure and success are both positive when you know how to deal with both. Your path will become steadier, and you will learn that your experiences are simply a journey. Life and sports are all about how you deal with it. You can mold yourself into a successful competitor with good information. When your competition time is over, you want to know you were a complete player mentally and physically and your time was well spent. Good competition will also make you a better person.

You will learn how to succeed. Once you know the process, it can work for anything you want to take on. This will work for full-time students or workers. Ten to twenty hours a week of dedication will take you to levels that you may have always just dreamed of. Be willing to make changes. Little steps make big things happen. Learn how to be mentally strong and confident. Stay on a positive path. It is all up to you. Have the never-give-up attitude. Honor and respect yourself and others.

When you are in the ZONE, competition and life can be a walk in the park. This information will help you get in the ZONE and stay in it for longer amounts of time. You will learn how to deal with the ups and downs of sports in a more positive and productive way. The goal is to reach your highest potential while always ENJOYING YOUR JOURNEY.

PHYSICAL PRACTICE

In the beginning, practice is an extremely important part of reaching your highest potential. You will not improve very much or very quickly if you do not put time and effort into it. Practice is where you put in the hard work, striving for perfection and excellence. Develop a practice plan, a daily plan, and a life schedule. Set some goals regularly.

A person that is willing to put in about ten hours per week of quality physical practice will excel at their sport at a very rapid pace. No wasted time. Think through new moves or shots, and work at getting better at and/or mastering the various skills of your sport. A larger percentage of your practice time should be spent on your weaker points. As an example, if you are a right-handed basketball player, you should dribble with your left hand most of the time during practice. Practice is about making your physical motions feel natural. Work harder on weak parts of your game, and your entire game will improve.

MAKING PHYSICAL CHANGES is not an easy process. Making changes is a very important subject when it comes to improving and reaching your highest potential. If you are fortunate enough to be taking private lessons, you must value them. You must trust what your teacher is teaching and work hard at making the changes necessary to improve your game. If you do not trust your teacher, get a different one. Students tend to hang on to what is OLD and FAMILIAR. It is so easy to do what is comfortable or go back to what was comfortable. If this is your mind-set, you are wasting time. IF YOU DO WHAT YOU HAVE ALWAYS DONE, YOU WILL GET WHAT YOU HAVE ALWAYS GOTTEN. The only way to improve is to change physical habits from not-so-good ones to the correct ones. Make the correct moves part of you. If you are not willing to CHANGE, you WILL NOT IMPROVE. Changes are made during lessons and practice. Suggestions on how to make physical changes will be presented later in this section.

Lessons and teachers are a part of you reaching your highest potential. Professionals take lessons. Lessons should be never ending. You must really focus on new changes and have a strong desire to improve your physical game. It is fairly common now for a professional golfer to have a physical teacher, a practice coach, a sports psychiatrist, and/or a mentor. Have teachers and listen to them.

THERE ARE A LOT OF PEOPLE WHO JUST DO NOT REALIZE WHAT IT REALLY TAKES TO COMPETE AT A PROFESSIONAL LEVEL. PROFESSIONALS MAKE THINGS LOOK EASY. IT IS NOT EASY TO REACH THE HIGH LEVELS.

LEARN. PRACTICE. CORRECTIONS. CHANGE. MORE PRACTICE.

A young gymnast aspiring to make it to an Olympic team will practice four to six or more hours per day, four to six days per week. This amount of time is simply what it takes for gymnasts to reach the highest levels of this sport. These athletes basically carry about 4% to 6% body fat. Gymnasts are amazing. The gymnast is really a great example of a very disciplined athlete. The gymnast must have about as perfect a body as one can have, and they must have their mental game, their mind, in exactly the right place to succeed.

The gymnast practices many long, hard hours and then has competitions every so often. Their performances are a very short amount of time. Every single move they make is critical. It takes a lot of patience and discipline to become accomplished at this sport.

There are extremes of practicing. There is one particular professional golfer who hit balls until her hands bled. That is an extreme. She was somewhat successful at the beginning of her career and really inspired many others to golf. At a fairly young age, she was burned out and took a long break. She is currently on tour again. Her practice methods have become more reasonable. In this case, practice was really overdone because it caused a burnout. It is important to work hard and pace yourself. To become excellent at anything, it does become a job, but the job should be enjoyable. Don't forget, you are doing what you love, don't overdo it so that you begin to dislike what you are doing.

If you have very little time to practice, decide if it is better for you to practice a little each day, or one or two big blocks of time in a week-long period. Usually, it is better to practice more often. Practicing is about developing physical habits. If you work on something every day, you are actually training your body to have your actions become natural and regular. The more you can FEEL like what you are doing is part of you, the better you will perform. It is good to work on one skill for a certain length of time. Repeating motions over and over trains our muscles to memorize.

One theory called the muscle memorization theory says that if you can repeat something thirty times in a row, your muscles will memorize it. Once your muscles have memorized a motion, your body will automatically come through for you when you need to do it without conscious thought. We will go over this more in the mental practice chapter because you are also training your mind when repeating physically.

With little time to practice, try attempting to repeat a motion at least nine out of ten times. Sometimes it may take as many as five or six attempts to get to nine out of ten. That is very similar to doing something thirty times in a row. You can also go one round of ten with one skill and other rounds of ten with other skills. This all depends on how many things you want to work on and the time you have to practice. This method will tell you easily about the percentage that you are successful. Five out of ten is 50%; nine out of ten is 90%. Knowing you can be 90% successful at a skill is a big plus for your mental confidence. Repeating anything thirty times in a row during practice or competition is a big number and a great goal. I was fortunate to have a conversation with EARL ANTHONY, a National Hall of Fame bowler with forty-one titles, and he explained this theory to me. He said he was a professional baseball pitcher and suffered a career-ending injury, so he took up bowling. He practiced forty games per day, across twenty lanes or so, every day for four years. This man had TIME to attempt to do something thirty times in a row. His theory worked for him. He was very successful on the professional tour. This is a great theory, and it can be modified to fit you and still work. Have a realistic practice plan with set goals for the time that you have to practice.

Practicing and the amount of time you practice depend on many factors. If you want to practice two to four hours a day, you must schedule your time. Most people are going to school or work. Consider practice your fun time. Get the daily chores done, and then get to the fun.

Think positively about having to schedule your time, as most athletes have to juggle time in order to get life and their sport done each day.

If you are fortunate enough to only have your sport to do, it is truly a luxury. Most of your time is available to dedicate to what you love to do, especially that forty-hour workweek or school that most have to put in. If you want to do it, you can do it. Simply HAVE A PLAN. IF YOU FAIL TO PLAN, YOU PLAN TO FAIL.

QUALITY PRACTICE: If you are serious about what you are doing, NEVER WASTE A SHOT. Do not waste time or opportunities to improve.

Practice is precious time. SELF-MOTIVATION has a lot to do with how much and how seriously you practice. If you are on a team, be the first one to practice and the last one to leave.

PRACTICE IS EXTREMELY IMPORTANT. PRACTICE IS TRAINING YOUR BODY to accept what you are doing as a NATURAL part of you. The more natural and comfortable you feel doing it, the better you will perform. Develop a routine.

ROUTINE is an important part of success, going through all the same motions over and over. How you put your shoes on, how you prepare your equipment, how you fix your hair, socks, etc. Move around at a slow and comfortable pace. Stretch out, smartly and slowly, warming and loosening up your body. For an individual practice session, know before you get to practice what you will be working on. Get your notebook out. Go to work.

Now it is time to work on something serious and/or intricate—developing a new skill, making a change, or working on current ones like the timing of skills such as swinging a golf club or shooting a basketball.

An example of practicing a current skill and timing is three hundred basketball shots. Start about five feet away, shoot ten from that distance, feel your timing, pay attention to form, and keep track of makes and misses. Five shooting positions is one recommended way to do this. Right side-R wing-center-Left wing-L side five feet, then move back to ten feet, then fifteen feet, then to twenty feet or three-point line. This adds up to two hundred shots. Follow with ten free throws, ten R-side layups, ten free throws, ten L-side layups—repeat, then twenty more free throws for three hundred shots. It is very likely that any high-scoring professional basketball player has had a routine like this for years and continues that same routine into their professional career. This is done at a time other than team practice time.

The pre-shot or pre-action routine is another important subject to be aware of and to handle while practicing. These routines can be used in many situations. This is just what you do BEFORE you do. Again, this is part of developing patterns so that what you do feels like a part of you, like walking feels to you. This is the goal. You want what you do to feel just as usual to you as walking, talking, sleeping, or sitting. Part of making what you do feel natural is to repeat, repeat, and repeat. So a pre-routine is very important.

Examples are what a pole-vaulter does just before the vault or what a free throw shooter in basketball does just before the free throw. For the free throw shooter, something like this should be done: take the ball from the referee, set feet, bounce ball twice, bend knees, focus on basket, take a deep breath for relaxation—shoot. This is an example of a pre-shot or pre-action routine to be repeated over and over. This routine assists you to perform mentally and physically. It is to help you become extremely FOCUSED on your task at hand. Develop pre-action routines, and remain very serious about them. This is an extremely important part of successful execution. Repeating the pre-shot routine is as important as the actual shot.

CHECKLISTS are another important part of a routine to develop for practice and competition. Checklists also assist you during competition when you have made a recent physical change. Checklists are a preaction mental list for actions—such as a free throw, a golf swing, a putt, a vault, a gymnastic routine, a free kick in a game of soccer, a swing of the bat—or possibly just before a team game such as basketball or football starts. The checklist is your conscious reminder, telling your body what it WILL DO. During practice, you can develop your personal checklist for your skills. This is what you would think just before execution. You are basically telling yourself, consciously, what you are going to do. These can also be physical reminders, short one-word phrases that mean something to you. Saying this checklist to yourself just before you begin your particular motions assists you with focus and is a reminder to yourself of what your body is going to do. Very importantly, your mind is telling your body what it WILL do. This pushes all negative conscious thought out of the mind. Zero negative thought is the goal.

Example, a bowling checklist: Body and ball are set up and ready to go. In your mind, say to yourself, PUSH, SLOW, LET, THROUGH. Breathe in, out, go. PUSH means push the ball away strong; SLOW to keep feet slow—timing reminder; LET means let it swing, stay relaxed; and THROUGH means follow through. It is thought in the order that it will be executed. In practice and during lessons is when your pre-shot routine and your checklist can be figured out. It is a good idea to change your checklist often. It keeps you paying attention to the correct things or a new change in your game. If you are competing in an individual sport, you will always be working on something. If you are in a team sport, you will always be working on better and new moves and routines, and checklists would be used differently for team sport athletes. Checklists keep your mind focused on competition. When your checklist involves one new reminder, this assists you in keeping focused on that one skill and allows you to let the rest of it happen because the rest is already ingrained in your game.

You can always get better, and if you are constantly working on something for improvement, a checklist helps keep you focused on what you are doing with all the parts of your game. Working on one particular change keeps all the positive parts of your game repeating because you are not thinking about them; you are just thinking about the one thing you are working on, and everything else is just there, part of you.

Routines and checklists are important and should be part of your practice so they happen automatically when you are competing.

DEVELOPING FEEL is another very important necessity for improvement and having the ability to make changes. You must learn to be aware of what your body is doing and know what it is doing even if you cannot see it. This is a skill that can be developed with good guidance and practice. It takes work, focus, patience, discipline, and knowledge to develop great FEEL.

First you must know the correct movement to feel. This varies from sport to sport. Example: if the backswing of a golf club is going past parallel at the height of your backswing, and you want to get it more parallel to the ground at the top of the swing, you will have to learn to FEEL the difference between them. Someone watching you will be of help. You cannot see this unless you swing in a mirror. If you do swing in a mirror, you are not getting the exact feeling because normally, you would be looking down at your ball throughout your swing. Developing feel and making changes go together for the most part.

DEVELOPING FEEL IS A CRITICAL PART OF MAKING CHANGES.

With someone watching, you would take your club back as you do normally and stop it at the top of your swing. HOLD THAT POSITION. FEEL IT. And then the helper will tell you where your club is compared to parallel with the ground. You would then take a backswing and stop it when you FEEL it is parallel to the ground. Then the helper will tell you where it is. Likely, the club will have passed parallel on your first attempt even though it *feels* to you as if it is parallel to the ground. If you don't believe your observer, you can take a visual check when you are stopped at what you "feel" is the desired position for your change. You must repeat the backswing, continuing to restrict your swing until the helper tells you the club is parallel to the ground when you stop your swing at the height of the backswing. NOW YOU KNOW WHAT IT FEELS LIKE FOR YOUR CLUB TO BE PARALLEL TO THE GROUND AT THE TOP OF YOUR BACKSWING.

A HINT: You will likely feel like you have hardly taken a backswing to get it to actually be parallel to the ground. You will really have to *exaggerate* what you feel for the backswing to get it where you want it to be. It will, at first, feel like a one-half or three-fourths backswing. Then you will do your normal swing, back, and stop. FEEL WHERE IT IS. Then execute the new swing. STOP, FEEL IT, CHECK WITH HELPER, and so on. You absolutely must continue this process WITHOUT hitting the ball until you can KNOW and FEEL the difference between the OLD backswing and the NEW and DESIRED backswing. Once you can feel the difference on the stopped backswing, then you begin to take a full swing with follow-through. Every swing, YOU MUST FEEL THAT SAME FEEL that is telling you your club is parallel to the ground. DO NOT GO BACK TO THE OLD SWING AT THIS POINT NO MATTER WHAT!

As your helper watches you take your full swings, you need to know after each swing if the club was parallel with the ground at the height of your backswing. As your helper sees it, YOU FEEL IT. Now you go to the muscle memorization theory. Attempt to take ten full swings, and get your desired position with the club. Keep track of how many times out of ten that you get the club in the correct place. Your helper will count. You just take your swings. When you're done, your helper will give you the report. It is very likely you will have gotten the desired swing three to five times out of ten. The rest will be close, and likely none of them will be as over swung as your old swing.

Once you have taken ten full swings and you get a count of nine or ten of ten, you get to attempt to hit the ball with your NEW SWING. If you follow this process when you hit your first ball, you will very likely see an immediate difference in your ball flight and FEEL a difference in the way the club sounds when it hits the ball. REMEMBER, what you are looking for is change and a difference. IT DOES NOT MATTER WHERE THE BALL GOES AT THIS POINT. While you are focusing on a new change and making it part of your game, other parts may go awry. JUST MASTER THE CHANGE and THE NEW FEEL for now, then go back to putting it all together, and the new part should be there for you. You should feel a different backswing at this point, and you will see a difference in ball flight and the sound of the club hitting the ball should be different. You should be able to feel the differences between the over swing and the new swing parallel to the ground. When this is achieved, you now have the ability to ingrain the new and desired motion into your game, so it also becomes a part of you and your game. Correctly done, it feels smooth and natural, and when the error is made, in this case an over swing, you can definitely feel the error. If an error is made in competition, on the next swing, FOCUS on the checklist and execute the new, good swing. This is your best chance and the best way to correct an error on your next swing.

By following this procedure, it will not take you long to incorporate the new FEEL and CHANGE into your game. Once you feel pretty good about your new change, you can now go back to your usual procedure and CHECKLIST for hitting the ball and GO FOR IT! The number of swings you take to develop this new feel depends on the individual. As you learn to feel, the process for new changes and feel will go faster.

You may now have a new CHECKLIST that incorporates a word that will remind you before you swing to keep the backswing restricted. The word may even be RESTRICT, HOLD, or SLOT for a one-syllable word. Your old checklist may have been something like STILL, SLOW, RELAX, and THROUGH, and your new checklist would become SLOW, HOLD, DOWN, and RELEASE. It is your checklist, so make one that works for you. Three to four one-syllable words work well when making changes. When you are very comfortable with your game, you may only have a ONE-WORD CHECKLIST. It may be RELAX, BREATHE, SLOW, or STILL. Now don't expect miracles, but you will have made a significant change in only one practice session. You continue each practice session with this procedure until your new motion is part of your game, and if you happen to whip out the old overswing, you will really FEEL it. When this happens, go back to that CHECKLIST to remind yourself before you swing to get back to what you want to do. Do not get angry or frustrated. Simply FOCUS ON THE CHECKLIST.

Being able to FEEL what is going on behind you is EXTREMELY CRITICAL for making changes and improving at just about any sport you attempt to reach a high level at. Being able to FEEL that you are balanced and stable is CRITICAL. A player that looks and/or plays out of control is not staying balanced. BALANCE and FEELING BALANCED is critical in all sports. If you FEEL balanced and in control, this is a good feeling. This, in many cases, means your TIMING is good to great. The best way to control this is do what you can while staying in control of your body. When your body gets out of control or you attempt to do something beyond your abilities without practice, disaster can strike.

Disaster has many meanings. Here are some examples of athletes getting out of balance and/or control: a skier will fall, a gymnast will have a poor routine or fall, a basketball player will miss the basket when shooting, a pole-vaulter will not make the jump, a golfer will not hit the ball well if at all, a motorcycle racer will crash, and a kicker in football will miss the field goal attempt. FEELING and being AWARE of your body, what it is doing, and being BALANCED and in TIME are VERY CRITICAL parts of reaching your fullest potential. In order to achieve great and/or PERFECT TIMING takes a lot of practice. REPEAT, REPEAT, REPEAT, and REPEAT some more.

The reward for learning to make changes and practicing and achieving the ability to FEEL perfect TIMING and BALANCE is SUCCESS and a feeling that you are DOING NOTHING AND GETTING EVERYTHING. These are the MOMENTS you are in THE ZONE. Your body and mind are working together. This happens for great athletes regularly. The goal is to be in the zone often. When you get in THE ZONE, it is AWESOME.

No matter what age you are and what sport you want to excel at, if you can put in about two hours per day, five or six days a week of QUALITY practice, you are going to pass a lot of people that you compete with or against. Almost anyone could break into the top 10% of anything in their age group and arena if they put this much time into it. Then when you go on to the next age group and arena, you will be right there with the rest of the best. Yes, if you work this hard, you will do better than 90% of all other people that do it too. If you practice thirty minutes per day, five or six days a week, you will probably outdo about 70% to 90% of others. I am talking about everybody, and everybody doesn't practice. IF IT WERE EASY, EVERYBODY WOULD BE DOING IT.

What happens when you reach the top 10%? Now you're starting to get into a more elite group. So to get into the upper 9% and so on, the steps become tougher and slower. After all that practice and passing lots of others, you start catching the better and the best. This is when the going gets tough. This is when your experience and your mental game really start coming into play.

The other factor that is important about practice is that you do have specific skills to work on. Usually this takes a teacher/coach to guide you. Always have a teacher. You will always have things to work on in practice because of those teachers. If you are serious about what you are doing, you really should be taking some sort of private lessons. Even if you are involved in a team sport, private lessons can help you develop your personal skills for that sport. A good teacher can give a team sport athlete many different skills and drills to practice on their own. If you are involved in an individual sport, private lessons are absolutely mandatory. You simply cannot advance up into the top 10% on your own in an individual sport. You will get better to some degree on your own, but you will never reach your highest potential without help. It has been said over and over again by many great people: NO ONE BECOMES SUCCESSFUL WITHOUT A MENTOR AND/OR HELP FROM OTHERS.

Finding the correct help is another subject. Be careful of whom you choose as a teacher. Get recommendations; do some research. If you are not comfortable with your choice, keep looking. When you do take a lesson, take advantage of it. Listen to everything, attempt to do what is being taught, and trust the lesson. If you are paying for it, this person should know more than you know. Use what you get that makes sense to you and feels comfortable and throw the rest away. Write down everything that you learn for future reference. Something you chose not to use currently may come in handy later. You may have to travel to find a teacher. The better you get, the harder a good teacher is to find. Some people even go out of their own state or country for lessons.

If you are a student athlete, respect your teachers and coaches. They are there for you and often are volunteering their time. The joy they get from teaching is often their only reward. Pay attention, work hard, and say thank-you.

The ability to compete only lasts so long. Value your time and learn as much as you can as quickly as you can. These are the keys to physical practice:

1. Practice an appropriate amount of time. A minimum of one to two hours per day, six days per week is recommended for the serious competitor.
2. Have a coach or teacher so you are learning and have specific practice goals. Be willing to make changes. Respect your teachers.
3. Have a practice plan. Have a routine before you begin practice. Your prepractice routine is actually part of practice. Think quality practice. Give your best.

4. Work on a specific skill until you can do it at least nine out of ten times or up to thirty times in a row. This lets your muscles and your mind memorize your motions and helps make them a natural part of you. Repeat, repeat, and repeat some more.

5. KEEP NOTES ON YOUR PRACTICE. This allows you to look back and see your progress, which helps build your confidence; this is a large part of preparation. Since confidence is knowing you are prepared, you really want to keep track of your preparation and successes during preparation.

6. Develop a PRESHOT/PREACTION ROUTINE and a CHECKLIST, and use them during practice and competition.

7. Work on FEEL. Feel balanced and stable. Feel correct as opposed to incorrect movements. The ability to feel what your body is doing helps you have the ability to correct physical mistakes during competition.

8. Most importantly, using PATIENCE and DISCIPLINE during practice is extremely critical.

9. Strive for perfection and excellence during practice. Work hard. Maintain a positive attitude.

10. Remember that feeling nothing and getting everything is perfect timing, and great timing brings great rewards.

11. Always remember how important practice is. Practice is part of your experience.

Note: Take practice seriously. DON'T WASTE TIME. Here is some food for thought about how difficult it is to obtain the perfect balance between self and doing.

THE PERFECT COMBINATION OF PHYSICAL AND MENTAL COMBINED is when you feel like you are doing nothing and you are GETTING EVERYTHING!

THE GREAT DUAL BURDEN OF EMOTION AND HIGH INTELLIGENCE IS SINGULAR TO HUMANKIND, AND IT IS WHAT MAKES LIFE SO HARD.

ALWAYS THINKING ABOUT WHAT YOU WERE FEELING INSTEAD OF JUST GOING WITH THE MOMENT, OR YOU WERE ALWAYS TRYING TO FEEL WHAT YOU THOUGHT YOU SHOULD FEEL IN A GIVEN SITUATION.

THOUGHTS AND JUDGMENT ARE INEVITABLY COVERED BY EMOTIONS, SOME ON A SUBCONSCIOUS LEVEL, SO YOU DIDN'T EVEN ENTIRELY UNDERSTAND WHY YOU MADE CERTAIN DECISIONS AND ACTED IN CERTAIN WAYS.

EMOTIONS CLOUD YOUR THINKING, BUT THINKING TOO HARD ABOUT YOUR FEELINGS TAKES THIS EDGE OFF. TRYING TO FEEL DEEPLY AND THINK PERFECTLY CLEAR AT THE SAME TIME IS LIKE SIMULTANEOUSLY JUGGLING SIX INDIAN CLUBS WHILE RIDING A UNICYCLE BACKWARD ALONG A HIGH WIRE.

OBVIOUSLY, IT WILL TAKE TIME AND EXPERIENCE TO ACHIEVE THIS.

Three basketball players looking to take on something different. They don't look to confident with a little different equipment in their hands.

Damond is looking very confident and happy. He traveled the US and Internationally with the Harlem Globtrotters. He spends 20 to 30 hours weekly coaching the youth and playing basketball. His new dream is to build a basketball academy for children in the Sacramento CA, area. Damond says, "There is no substitute for hard work. Success, Confidence and Luck follow."

PRACTICE CHARTS

IF YOU FAIL TO PLAN, YOU PLAN TO FAIL, and keeping track of your practice is part of the plan. KNOWLEDGE EQUALS NO FEAR, and when you keep track of your practice, you learn about yourself, your strengths and weaknesses, what you need to work on more, and what to work on less. KNOWING YOUR GAME is part of KNOWING YOURSELF, and when you chart your practice, your strong and weak points GLARE AT YOU from the notes. By charting your skills as you practice them, the IMPROVEMENT will GLARE AT YOU, and this will build your CONFIDENCE. CONFIDENCE IS KNOWING YOU ARE PREPARED. If you track your skills and see your improvement, this shows you all that you have done to PREPARE. You KNOW YOU ARE AS PREPARED AS YOU CAN BE, and therefore, there is not one reason to be anything but CONFIDENT that you can and will go out and give it your best. With NO EXPECTATIONS, take what you get and go on.

These are some examples of how to chart certain skills. You can take one of these examples and make up your own ways to chart the skills that you practice for your particular sport.

BASKETBALL SHOOTING PRACTICE

FEET/SPOT	MISS/MAKES	% MADE	TOTAL SHOTS	TOTAL %
5-10-15 R Baseline	6/10-5/10-4/10	60%-50%-40%	15/30	50%
5-10-15' R Wing	8/10-6/10-6/10	80%-60%-60%	20/30	66%
5-10-15' F Center	7/10-8/10-5/10	70%-80%-50%	20/30	66%
5-10-15' L Wing	6/10-5/10-4/10	60%-50%-40%	15/30	50%
5-10-15' L Baseline	5/10-5/10-5/10	50%-50%-50%	15/30	50%
	5' 10' 15'			
TOTALS	32/50-29/50-24/50	64%-58%-48%	85/150	56%

This gives you an idea of how to keep your NUMBERS. Numbers and percentages have a lot to do with sports. Statistics have a lot to do with sports. Knowing you have good numbers will build your confidence. If you don't know how to figure out percentages, LEARN HOW TO DO IT. Any math teacher will be glad to show you. HARD WORK DOES EQUAL SUCCESS. WORK HARD. A professional basketball player will make about 95% to 100% of his/her shots when there is no defense on them. This converts to about 35% to 50% for games. A professional that averages 40% to 50% from the floor for games is considered a great shooter. Think about this. This is a 50% to 60% rate of FAILURE, yet this is considered successful. Please understand that competition is not about BEING PERFECT.

EXAMPLES OF A PRACTICE CHART

BASKETBALL

	Made/Attempts 5'	M/A 10'	M/A 15'	M/A 20	M/A 3-pt. line	TOTALS-%
R Baseline	8-10	7-10	6-10	4-10	4-10	29/50-58%
R Wing						
Center						
L Wing						
L Baseline						
Totals-%						

GOLF

	Made/Attempts	M/A	M/A	M/A	M/A	TOTALS-%
3' putt						
5' putt						
10' putt						
Uphill 5'						
Downhill 5'						
Totals-%s						

These are ideas to get you going on charting practice sessions. Make one up the way you like it. Make blank copies and use them during practice. Later, figure out your percentages. As you practice and get better, you will see improvement, which will build your confidence, and this will also give you knowledge of what you can and can't do. Always work harder on your weak spots. Using practice charts gives you a big advantage on learning about yourself as an athlete. Some of the greatest golfers have a laptop with them at practice.

EQUIPMENT

Equipment is an essential part of your sport. It may seem simple, for example, to go play some tennis. You do need a few things to play after you find a court to play on. You will need a racket and tennis balls, for starters. For comfort, you should have a good pair of tennis shoes, shorts, and a comfortable loose-fitting shirt. This is what you would need just to go out and have some fun. As you get more serious about this sport, you will need more equipment.

Some sports don't really involve too much equipment while others require a lot of equipment, especially at high levels. Basketball does not require very much equipment. You basically need a basketball, a good pair of athletic shoes, a pair of comfortable shorts, and a loose-fitting T-shirt. Sports such as bowling or golf require a lot of equipment. Golf may just be the most expensive sport considering equipment. For an amateur, it can cost anywhere from $300 to more than $2,000 for a complete set of clubs with a bag. Bowling balls can cost $50 to over $300 each. An amateur usually uses two bowling balls. A professional bowler may use eight to twelve bowling balls or more during a season. Professional bowlers and golfers constantly change and try new equipment to help improve their competitions.

What you need to realize about equipment is that it can get expensive. When you purchase equipment for anything you are doing, you should know what you are doing. You can waste a lot of money on equipment without knowledge of equipment. Do not be afraid to ask for help from someone with knowledge about your sport. This is another good reason to take lessons. Your teacher should help you learn about the equipment necessary to assist you in achieving your highest potential. Equipment does not make a player. Equipment is a great tool for a great player who has already put in a lot of hard work and knows how to use that specialized equipment. Practice and hard work make a player. The proper equipment for a player adds another advantage and assist for competition.

- Equipment is a very important part of your sport.
- Equipment may be inexpensive for some sports.
- Equipment may be very expensive for some sports.
- Know what you are doing when you purchase equipment.
- Ask or learn from a professional.

- Equipment can greatly assist you in reaching your highest potential once you have developed the basic physical skills necessary for your sport.

DEALING WITH INJURY

INJURY IS BAD. INJURY CAUSES SETBACK. NO ONE WANTS AN INJURY.

Injuries never come at a good time. Anyone who follows sports knows injuries are devastating. They devastate the individual, and if that individual is on a team, it can devastate a team and it always devastates the fans.

When a hardworking athlete is injured, everything they have worked for comes to an immediate stop. Big-time injuries that immediately come into my mind are the following:

Chris Webber	NBA	KNEE	ACL
Joe Theismann	NFL	LEG	Broken
DeMya Walker	WNBA	KNEE	Tendon tear
Annika Sörenstam	LPGA	BACK	Discs
Michelle Wie	LPGA	WRIST	Ligaments
Dwyane Wade	NBA	SHOULDER	Tears
Amar'e Stoudemire	NBA	KNEE	ACL
Lance Armstrong	CYCLING	CANCER	
Edna Campbell	WNBA	CANCER	
Ruthie Bolton	WNBA	KNEE	ACL

Injuries to these people, some career ending, devastated the individual, their peers, their teams, and their fans. LET THESE PEOPLE BE YOUR INSPIRATION IF YOU SUFFER AN INJURY. THESE PEOPLE SHOULD BECOME YOUR NEW HEROES.

Joe Theismann's injury was career ending, and he is currently a commentator for football. DeMya Walker recovered from a torn patella tendon, and she continued her career in 2008. Dwyane Wade recovered from his surgery and was back for the 2008 NBA season. The rest of those mentioned are currently competing and healthy, or they have recovered, made great comebacks, and/or since retired from their respective sport.

If you are injured and you think about these athletes, they can motivate you. They are all great athletes; they went through the grueling and boring process of rehabilitation. This was not fun at all. They took all the little steps necessary to come back to their respective sports and continued with success. YES, two of them survived CANCER! If you are a great athlete, in most cases, nothing stops you. Great athletes prove that over and over again.

Most of these players got well and returned to their arena. There have been athletes that have been injured and were unable to continue their sport, and they went on and did a different sport or another type of competition. There have been some movies made about athletes like this. An excellent one about this is REMEMBER THE TITANS. It is very important to ALWAYS HAVE A BACKUP PLAN. One injury can end an athletic career. VALUE YOUR EDUCATION, and ALWAYS GIVE YOUR BEST AS A STUDENT. Be educated because you will need to be educated at some point.

Recovering from an injury will take all the drive, perseverance, patience, discipline, and heart that you have inside of you. You must follow directions and stick with your plan for recovery. Point-blank recovery from an injury sucks.

In the long run, it will make you better, stronger, and more confident if you deal with it correctly. Just think about it. You get to make stronger many of your other body parts that are not injured. That's a plus. You get to practice mental discipline and patience. You have to follow a strict schedule. You get to have time to think of ways you can improve. You will have time to read about and study your sport. Yes, use this time to improve your knowledge of your sport or knowledge of anything you want to read about.

Most importantly, DO NOT DO TOO MUCH, TOO SOON, TOO FAST. A step backward in this situation would not be a learning experience. (Well, you would learn that you better not push it.) It just would be more rehab and more work.

You must tell yourself you are getting stronger in many ways. You must tell yourself, "All this hard work will pay off, and when I come back, I will be even better than I was before." When and if you begin to doubt that, think about all your new heroes. All those athletes that came back and successfully continued their careers. You are no different than they are. It is up to you.

When an injury is devastating and negative, you can still make something positive of it. DeMya Walker said the only good thing about her injury was that she got to spend more time with her new baby girl. I'm sure that helps her mentally because I know it hurt big-time inside not to be able to play.

Unfortunately, injuries happen. You must go on. You must get through it. The most important thing is to be as positive as you can be. Then you will not lose your confidence when you return. When you return, you want to be as mentally and physically ready as possible so you will be confident.

Tell yourself over and over again, "I will be back, and when I get back, I will be stronger, smarter, and better than I was before."

MENTAL PRACTICES

THE ZONE

Wow, that kid has got IT! He is really in the ZONE! He is IN IT—phenomenal! Wow, they really make that LOOK EASY. Is this what you would love to know someone was saying about you or your team during your competition?

Mental practice, understanding how to train your subconscious mind, mental checklists, focus, and determination, combined with the physical parts of competition, are a large part of being successful. When all these are working together, this is when the possibilities are big for you to be in that ZONE. This means the mind and body are working together perfectly. YOU FEEL AS IF YOU ARE DOING NOTHING AND YOU ARE GETTING EVERYTHING! It is all feeling easy, feeling perfect. This is what athletes strive for, being in the ZONE. This is the time for PEAK PERFORMANCES. The athletes that seem to be in THE ZONE most of the time are the athletes that have themselves prepared physically, and they have their mind in the right place. Having your mind in the right place is extremely important. This chapter is particularly about what and how to think in several situations and about the importance of visualization.

Practicing in your mind, sometimes called visualization, is really a fairly easy task. You really can picture yourself going through routines and motions and repeat them over and over again in your mind. Your subconscious mind does not know the difference between practicing live or practicing mentally. When you practice repeating in your mind, it is PERFECT PRACTICE. You are doing everything perfectly, just as you would want to during physical practice and competition. The cool thing is, you can get a lot of practice with a little effort, and you can practice in many different places and situations.

Picturing different situations in your mind over and over, practicing a positive action and result, or picturing that one successful moment you strive for is REAL to your subconscious mind. The main idea is to train your subconscious mind with mental practice, and when the real situation is occurring, your body basically comes through for you because your subconscious mind "believes" and/or "knows" you can do it.

Have you ever heard an athlete say something like, it was exactly how I had dreamed it? Brian Boitano, an Olympic ice-skater, won his first gold medal and made a comment about his success like this: "I have dreamed this moment so many times, I am still not sure this is real." How many times do you think he went over his routines in his mind and pictured himself standing on the podium receiving an Olympic gold medal? It was likely hundreds of times.

Part of the reason he lived his perfect performance during the Olympic competition is he visualized it over and over again in his mind. His subconscious mind "KNEW" he could do it, and his conscious mind just LET IT HAPPEN! This is a great example of the conscious mind and the subconscious mind working together perfectly. Athletes must train their bodies and their minds and then LET IT perform. Negative conscious thought is what can mess up your performances.

This is a main key of GETTING OUT OF YOUR OWN WAY. You must get out of your conscious mind's way and LET YOUR TRAINED SUBCONSCIOUS mind do its thing. You must know that your body can do the job, and let yourself perform as you have visualized yourself doing over and over again. YOU CANNOT LET NEGATIVE THOUGHTS OR ANY NEGATIVE COMMENTS AFFECT YOU. YOU MUST PUSH ALL NEGATIVE THOUGHTS OUT OF YOUR MIND AND REPLACE THEM WITH POSITIVE THOUGHTS.

This is what FOCUS is all about! You must remain FOCUSED. FOCUS on the task at hand, do what you have been training to do, and DO NOT THINK during competition. LET IT HAPPEN! All the thinking, practice, hard work, preparation, learning, etc., is done before and after your competition time is over. When it is time to compete, GO OUT AND PLAY, ENJOY IT! With this exact ATTITUDE, you will reach your fullest potential much more often. Your performances will be much more consistent, and these consistent performances will allow you to call on yourself even more when you really need something extra. Being IN THE ZONE is an awesome and valuable experience.

PATIENCE AND DISCIPLINE must be a part of your mental game. Being patient and disciplined is developed in your mind. It is a mind-set. You must learn to be patient when working on new skills and repeating skills that you have mastered or at least can do well. All good things take time. Being disciplined means sticking with your practice plan. Take your time preparing for your practice. Take the time to warm up properly. Begin doing things you can do and then work on the things you can't do or don't do well. Finish your practice with something positive. Do not end practice after anything negative has happened. Your subconscious mind will remember things ended on a positive note. In order to compete at your best level, you must become disciplined, and the way you become disciplined during competition is to be disciplined during your practice time. This is a conscious mental decision, and you must decide to be disciplined in order to reach your highest potential.

Great athletes often talk about distractions. The bigger the event, the more distractions. Watch high-level athletes prepare for competition. They may start out by wearing headphones and listening to music. This helps keep distractions away. As they stretch out and loosen up, look at their faces. They look serious. They have their game face on. This is mental. This is being focused. They avoid eye contact with outsiders. They avoid conversation with outsiders. They are totally focusing on the event that is about to occur. They are clearing their mind of thought and simply preparing to compete.

You will see these athletes go through certain routines. Routines are part of the mental game. Their preparation to compete will be repetitive. It is important how you feel about yourself, how you look, how you put your uniform or attire on, what your number is, how your equipment looks and feels. It is even important to travel comfortably and stay in a comfortable environment. This is all part of the mental game. All these are very important for your personal preparation. You may think this is ridiculous or untrue. All these details matter, and they do make a difference. Patience and discipline are two extremely important mental skills that must be developed to assist an athlete in reaching their highest potential.

PATIENCE means you must be patient with yourself. You must allow yourself time to practice, improve, learn more, fail, succeed, fail, succeed, fail, succeed. This is reality, NOT A VIDEO GAME. Each plateau you reach takes time, practice, failure, and experience. You must focus and work hard, but keep the expectations out of it. When you are very competitive, it is easy to become frustrated with yourself. You can call yourself all kinds of names when you practice and compete. You might get angry at surroundings, at yourself, and at results you get. That is really very natural for most competitive people. This is the fuel that stokes the fire inside. It is about how you deal with that. Go ahead, call yourself an IDIOT! Get it over with. Then refocus; go back to your CHECKLIST and what you ARE GOING TO DO next. MOVE ON!

DISCIPLINE is mental and a factor of moving on. Keep the feelings of anger and frustration short, and push them away. Let it go and MOVE ON. This is a big part of being mentally disciplined. You have to know that "losing it" mentally is not going to benefit you. Looking and acting out of control is a huge negative. This is when the individual athlete will begin to stick out like a sore thumb. This does not create a positive reputation, and having a good reputation can be a great intimidation factor when competing. This is a big reason why so many athletes look so stoic. They are focusing on keeping their mind and body balanced in every way possible. A stoic and focused athlete can be very intimidating.

THE CHECKLIST is another must for your mental game. The checklist is a big KEY for the mental game, and this subject was covered in the "Physical Practice" section previously. The checklist is a valuable physical and mental tool necessary for success. A positive checklist keeps the negative thoughts out of your mind.

When you are practicing physically, this is the time you should plan and develop your mental and physical routines and your pre-action CHECKLIST.

For example, you are going to attempt a putt while golfing. There should be a personal pre-action routine and checklist developed. The pre-action routine may be something like this: remove putter from bag, walk around green to analyze, look in front and back of hole, picture your ball following your chosen line and dropping in the hole, approach ball, and set feet. The checklist might be something like this: SET—reminder of correct body posture, SWINGS—for two practice swings, RELAX—reminder to take a breath and relax, THROUGH—follow through.

You can create any routine you want to. Whatever that preshot routine is, it must be repeated over and over again. The checklist just before your action is very important. It goes like this in your mind: set, swings, relax, through—GO. Again, this is a positive thought process that is keeping all negative thoughts out of your mind. Never forget that if your muscles are not relaxed, it will cause misdirection. Relaxed muscles create room for error. It is extremely important to be relaxed during any competition. *Relax* is a great word for part of your checklist.

Putting is a very important part of golf. As the saying goes, "Drive for show, putt for dough." Putting is usually where the high-pressure situation occurs. What is going to help you most in making these critical putts, on a large scale, is what the whole subject of this book is. You are prepared, you have repeated this routine hundreds or thousands of times, you are confident. NO PRESSURE because you KNOW you can make putts. You make the putt. You can create these types of personal routines and checklists for anything. If the one you create doesn't work, create a new one.

The purpose of a CHECKLIST is to keep your conscious mind busy with positive conscious thought, not letting any negatives creep in and LETTING your body do what it KNOWS it can do. It is very likely that if you let the thought "What if I miss?" come into your mind, you will miss. It is important for every putt to mean the same to you. Do not think about it. Go through your pre-shot routine and do it. Always give your best effort to go through your routine, focus, and make the putt. The more you make, the more your subconscious and conscious minds know you can make putts. Confidence is knowing you are prepared. Knowledge equals NO FEAR.

For an individual sport such as golf, tennis, or bowling, these checklists are very important. For the tennis serve, a checklist might be UP, SEE, THROUGH. UP, reminding you of making the perfect toss up to yourself; SEE, meaning seeing the racket make contact with your ball correctly; and THROUGH, reminding you of your great and strong follow-through.

Again, the main reason for the CHECKLIST is to keep negative conscious thought out of your mind. Tell your body what it IS GOING TO DO, and then let your body do it.

One of the worst things that can happen is when a coach, friend, or whoever is telling you what not to do. Like, don't miss, don't think, don't slice it, etc. DON'T is a very negative word. If you hear that, put it right out of your mind and repeat your checklist over and over, push out the negative by telling yourself what YOU WILL DO. Negative thoughts truly affect your performances. It is easy to get mentally distracted, and your CHECKLIST is a big part of keeping you and your mind right where it needs to be to perform at your highest potential.

EMOTION and controlling it is another part of the mental game. The ability to control your emotions is a very good attribute to have. Athletes that can show their emotion and still perform at a superior level are a rare breed. Most athletes really need to keep all their emotions under strict control, or their performances start suffering. Stoic athletes can be boring to watch at times, but that is the way they must be for them. Watching the emotional athlete can be a lot more fun. It really isn't about the fan, but most fans love seeing the emotion come out. Watching a competition is usually more emotional than being in the competition. Feeling the emotion is really why fans watch. The experience of having all those emotions is a large part of being a fan and having a lot of fun as a fan. As an athlete, always appreciate the fans. Keep your own emotions in check. Getting too emotional can hurt your performance. You need to know and understand your own emotions. How emotions help or hurt your performances can be very individual. Pay attention to your emotions, and learn what is best for you as far as keeping them in check.

Emotions can be feelings of anger, disappointment, frustration, sadness, joy, etc. Too much anger wipes out your adrenaline and energy, and so does too much joy. It is usually best to hold on to the celebrations until the competition is over. Expressing emotion as an athlete can be detrimental in many different ways.

The negative emotions should be and are mostly experienced after competition. Feeling anger, frustration, or disappointment during competition can really defeat you and turn your performances into poor ones quickly. These feelings can destroy your drive, motivation, and heart. Work hard to push these emotions away while you are competing. Continue to stay positive, give your best, and finish with your head up.

Some disappointments can bring you to tears. You get over it and you go on. Failure and disappointments are always going to be part of the package. Dealing with these situations in athletics really helps you in life to deal with ups and downs. When considering emotions and ups and downs, this is part of our daily lives. As you deal with your emotions better with competition, it will also improve how you deal with all the life situations we face. When competing is dealt with correctly, it can wind up helping your life be much better. A good cry now and then never hurts. We must have the ability to release pain just as we express joy. Do your best to save your expression of emotions after the competition is over.

FEAR and INTIMIDATION are two more mental factors. To be afraid to go out and compete is not a good feeling. Remember, CONFIDENCE is KNOWING you are PREPARED, and KNOWLEDGE EQUALS NO FEAR. It is a fact that there is always someone better out there. As you progress as an athlete, you reach higher levels. If you have just moved up a notch, you are now at the bottom of the top again. You are now a ROOKIE. Accepting that the best is always out there somewhere is just a good way to help you to not be intimidated and/or afraid of your competition. The mind-set really has to be ALL I CAN DO IS MY BEST and I AM ONLY AS GOOD AS I AM. I WILL GO OUT AND DO IT AND TAKE IT FROM THERE. This mind-set can relieve a lot of pressure. FEAR will not get you anywhere. There is really nothing to be afraid of. You are doing what you love to do, GO FOR IT.

Here is an example for you. Let's say you are ranked sixtieth on the planet as a professional tennis player. You are inside of the upper 1% of tennis players on the planet. AWESOME. You are about to play in your first US OPEN. It just so happens that you are playing close enough to where you grew up that you will have a nice crowd of fans there to watch you. You have learned that your first match will be played against the fifteenth-ranked player. Is that enough to give someone the jitters? YES! First US OPEN, hometown fans, and facing a player ranked forty-five spots above you. WHEW! This could be a mental disaster.

This would be an appropriate thought process to assist in avoiding a mental disaster.

THINK POSITIVE. Think like this: I have worked very hard to get here. I am prepared, and confidence is knowing I am prepared. This is an opportunity to prove myself. It really doesn't matter if I win or lose. I will give my best. I will be focused, disciplined, and I will play my game. I will not let outside distraction bother me. I will enjoy having my friends and fans here. I am going to ENJOY this opportunity and make the most of it. Wow, the US OPEN. This will be GREAT!

A thought process like this will greatly decrease, if not eliminate, all feelings of fear, dread, jitters, and intimidation. If you begin to think one tiny negative thought, PUSH IT OUT with all the positive ones. There are many positive thoughts to think, so what would be the point of thinking negatively?

When mistakes are made, you cannot just say, "Oh well, I'll do it next time." You can't get angry about it. That's not the way you get to know yourself. You have to note the mistake or failure, and later, you grab it by the throat, face it, dissect it, and analyze it. You then turn that mistake into a positive. Those mistakes and failures are what you learn from. They are your TEACHERS and part of your VALUABLE EXPERIENCE. You cannot buy experience.

Many great athletes realize that they fail over and over again, and that is WHY THEY SUCCEED. This is a very important message. It will prove itself out to you as true over and over again. Think about this: If you bat 50%, that is very successful, but you are still FAILING five out of ten times. If you shoot 50% in a basketball game, it is considered great, but you are FAILING five out of ten times. Failure and success go together and work together. You cannot have success without failure. It is simply part of the deal. You might as well make it positive in your mind instead of negative.

Successes only show you what your potential is. Success creates EXPECTATION. There are sections dedicated to dealing with expectation and success.

WHEN YOU HAVE EXPECTATIONS, YOU ARE GIVING UP YOUR CONTROL OF THE SITUATION.

- CONFIDENCE, YES
- KNOWLEDGE, YES
- SKILLS, YES
- PRACTICE, YES
- PATIENCE AND DISCIPLINE, YES
- EXPECTATION, NO, NONE

Successes allow you to reach for higher goals. You have to analyze what your incorrect choices were. Ask yourself, what physical mistakes did I make? What brings improvement is analyzing your mistakes and facing your failures. This is another part of getting your mind and body together as one.

Mental and emotional mistakes are important to analyze. By facing your fears, analyzing your mistakes, understanding them, and not being afraid to make a mistake, the mistakes lessen and you gain knowledge, and KNOWLEDGE EQUALS NO FEAR.

The "NO FEAR" motto we see on shirts and stickers, well, do they know the answer to "HOW DO YOU BECOME FEARLESS?" The answer is simply KNOWLEDGE—knowledge of your sport and yourself. If you KNOW yourself, know your equipment, know your potential, and know your abilities, you will have NO FEAR! You will have a much more peaceful time competing than someone who does not have this knowledge. This is a big part of being one with your mind and your body. This is a big part of being the one to beat in a competition because you are no longer beating yourself. Now your competition has to beat you.

If you have no fear while competing, the chances are very high that you will be successful. The goal is competition after competition, one at a time, giving 100%

of yourself. This is another very important part of the mental game. The higher the level you go, the more important all this becomes in order to be successful. There is more pressure and expectation to be eliminated before you compete. All these factors add up to being more successful.

Pressure is something that you have to learn to deal with. If you don't, when it really counts, you will fold. Some of this is overcome with experience. Visualizing successful situations and training your subconscious mind can ease pressure situations. Your subconscious mind does not know the difference between reality and thought.

KEYS TO MENTAL PRACTICE

1. The ZONE. Understand what being in the ZONE is. This is where you want to be when competing as often as possible. The mind and body work together as one. Stay within your capabilities and stay within yourself. Know what you can and cannot do.
2. Train your subconscious mind so it can overtake your conscious mind during competition.
3. Learn and know that when the mind and body work perfectly together, it feels as if you are doing nothing and getting everything. The ZONE.
4. Practice visualization.
5. FOCUS: Focus on the moment, whether it is during practice or competition, physically and mentally.
6. Practice, know, and use CHECKLISTS.
7. REPEAT everything positive that is part of your game in your mind.
8. Be PATIENT and DISCIPLINED.
9. KNOW YOURSELF and your emotions, and keep yourself and your emotions under control.
10. Eliminate FEAR and INTIMIDATION by knowing you are PREPARED.
11. LET IT HAPPEN.
12. ALWAYS GIVE YOUR BEST and know that this is all that is within your CONTROL. Do not try to control what you cannot control.
13. KNOW THAT YOUR MENTAL GAME IS COMPLETELY DIFFERENT WHEN YOU PRACTICE AS COMPARED TO WHEN YOU COMPETE.

Practice is to improve, get rid of frustration, eliminate mistakes, work on what you can do well some, work on what you can't do well a lot, develop checklists, and repeat, repeat, and repeat some more. Mental practices reinforce all that you worked so hard on.

The competition is to ENJOY! SUCCEED, FAIL, FOCUS, USE YOUR CHECKLISTS, LET IT HAPPEN, HAVE FUN, SHOW YOUR HEART, BE IN THE ZONE, SHOW YOURSELF WHAT YOUR POTENTIAL IS, and LOVE IT EVERY SECOND because the ability to compete at a physical sport only lasts so long. Allow yourself to do what you can do, and enjoy the feeling of DOING NOTHING AND GETTING EVERYTHING because you have trained your mind and body to work together as ONE.

THIS IS THE ULTIMATE GOAL.

Jared and Ruthie are showing FOCUS and CONCENTRATION
with a strong shooting form.

GAME TIME

Your mental and physical game at practice is completely different from GAME TIME. Mental and physical practice has been thoroughly covered. Game time thinking as opposed to practice thinking is an important subject.

It is very tough, if not impossible, for anyone to practice with the same mind-set, feelings, and motivation that exist when competition time arrives. Let's face it—practice is the tough part and can even be boring and monotonous at times. The repetition, drills, running, weights—all the training is the hard work that gets us to THE GAME.

Game time is the exciting part. Finally, we get to go out and do it. It is normal to feel excited, have some butterflies, and feel anticipation. It is kind of like going on a new big ride at an amusement park. You just don't know what you are going to get, but you know it is going to be fun. You just can't wait to get to it. When the competition begins, these feelings usually go away and adrenaline takes over. Adrenaline is what must be controlled and paced. At the end of the competition, you may need some of your adrenaline to give you that "something extra" you need to succeed.

You will often see a not-so-good athlete or team start out great against a better opponent. You may find yourself thinking, what is wrong with that guy or that team? That is the weaker opponents' adrenaline being used. Weaker opponents normally "psyche up" against greater opponents. The better athlete or team is very prepared and confident. The better opponents stick to their game plan, pacing themselves, and, in the end, are usually successful. Little by little, the better athlete or team catches and passes the weaker athlete or team. This is what the saying "The cream always rises to the top" means.

Individual competitions such as golf, bowling, and tennis are done over a long period of time, involving many rounds, games, or matches. Golf is usually two to four rounds of eighteen holes over a two-to four-day period. Bowling is twenty-eight to fifty-six games over a two- to four-day period. Tennis is three to five sets of matches against one opponent in a bracket format with several matches necessary to reach the finals over a period of two to five or more days. Quite often, the stars or higher-seeded athletes will start out behind. The greater opponents pace themselves mentally and physically while the weaker opponents use up their adrenaline early.

When it is time for that extra effort needed at the end, the greater athlete has adrenaline left to use because they have stayed calm and steady throughout the competition. This is when the "cream" begins to rise above and to the top.

If you pay attention to high-level and professional competitions, you will see this situation occur over and over again. Knowing you need to learn how to pace yourself physically and mentally is very important. Experience is also part of the price you must pay to become a great athlete. Experience will teach you to pace yourself. It is important to be aware of your use of adrenaline so you can learn to control it. Learning to compete with a steady aggressiveness and, in the end, leaving everything in you out there will take time and experience. Here are some examples for you to watch for the "cream rising to the top":

1. An unranked college football team playing against a top twenty-five team
2. Any last place team playing against a top one to fourth place team
3. A lower ranked tennis player or golfer playing against a top ten ranked player

When you are going into game time, everything matters. Look good, feel good, and play well. Limit outside distractions, focus on your warm-up, and keep your mind still.

IT'S GAME TIME.

PUT ON YOUR GAME FACE.

FOCUS.

BE INTENSE.

BE IN CONTROL OF YOURSELF MENTALLY AND PHYSICALLY.

SHOW YOUR STUFF; DO YOUR THING.

BE CONFIDENT; YOU KNOW YOU ARE PREPARED.

PACE YOURSELF.

LEAVE IT ALL OUT THERE.

PLAY AS IF IT IS THE LAST TIME YOU WILL EVER PLAY.

HAVE A BLAST.

In my book, there is nothing better than good, clean competition.

TREASURE IT.

ALWAYS ENJOY YOUR JOURNEY.

EXPECTATION AND PRESSURE

Having EXPECTATIONS is negative.

Feeling PRESSURED is negative.

If you EXPECT something, you are giving away YOUR control of YOUR situation.

A very important mental approach involving competition and/or life is CONTROL WHAT YOU CAN CONTROL AND DO NOT ATTEMPT TO CONTROL WHAT YOU CANNOT CONTROL.

Attempting to control something you know you cannot control is a complete waste of time and energy mentally and physically. Spend your time and energy working on things that are within your control. Frustration will be felt far less with this approach.

When you EXPECT things, you are giving up your control mentally. When a person works hard, they almost naturally EXPECT RESULTS. It is true that hard work pays, but to EXPECT payoffs is not a positive way to think about it. All good things take time, and rewards for hard work come in little by little, in most cases. Large, fast rewards can be detrimental and create huge expectation. Remember, it is better for the waves of sports and life to go up and down in small increments. It is truly better for resumes to be built slowly and steadily. Don't ever forget about all the others that are out there, working hard to succeed. There will always be someone better out there, and a competitor can be humbled very quickly. You must learn to go into competitions with NO EXPECTATIONS. EXPECT NOTHING.

43

Others can create expectation for you also, and you must be aware of this. Parents, friends, and fans will have expectations of you. Comments made to you about those expectations can really put pressure on you to perform. You must not let those comments affect your mind-set. The appropriate thought is to tell yourself that you are prepared and ready to go out and give YOUR BEST. Your answer to those comments should be something like, "I'll be giving it my best."

When you allow yourself to begin a competition with a lot of expectation, it will affect you physically. Stop and think right now about two different mind-sets. First, try to FEEL what it feels like to be full of expectation to win an event. Close your eyes and picture yourself at your next competition. Tell yourself, "I expect to win this" or "I know our team will win." Tell yourself, "Everyone knows I/we will win, and they expect it." Try to feel what you will feel like beginning that competition with all this expectation in your mind. The competition begins. Try to feel what this would feel like: You get behind. NOW WHAT? The very FIRST thing you are going to feel is PRESSURE. Feeling PRESSURE affects you physically in a negative way. Your relaxed body tightens up, and your performance worsens. Then PANIC sets in. Can you FEEL it? Do you get the idea?

Second, try feeling and thinking this way: tell yourself, "I have worked hard, I am prepared, and I am confident because I know I am prepared. I am ready to go out and give it my best. The only thing I will do is to leave it all out there and fight to the finish. May the best win."

You get behind. No pressure. Just keep playing and giving it your best. No panic. No failure. Give your best and the final score does not matter. Giving your best is success.

THIS IS WHAT COMPETITION IS! This is all competition should ever be. Prepare, go to battle, and have fun. Take what you get and go on. IT IS REALLY SO SIMPLE, but some of us make it so ugly and difficult. Try to FEEL the difference of the two thought processes, just sitting and thinking them through. The thought and feeling of EXPECTATION versus the thought and feeling of KNOWING you are PREPARED and CONFIDENT to compete are TWO DIFFERENT WORLDS. The more you learn to let go of expectation of any kind and only think about the fact that you are ready and know you will give your best, the better and more consistent positive results you will get. Having and using this thought process will also greatly assist you in dealing with your failures and the disappointments that come with failure.

When a person feels PRESSURE, they begin to PANIC. DO NOT PANIC! You are playing a game, a sport. This same scenario can happen in life situations also. MISTAKES will always be made. Without mistakes, you cannot IMPROVE. Without NEGATIVES, there cannot be POSITIVES. When mistakes are made, you must keep your head up and keep going. No one plays perfectly. Many players are motivated by mistakes. You will often see a good athlete make a mistake and then immediately follow up with a great play. Accept mistakes as part of the game. Keep PLAYING, have FUN, and enjoy the competition.

NOTE THIS: As observers of events, we hear a lot of "Wow, that player can really perform UNDER PRESSURE. He/she really has IT. That player always GETS IT DONE." The TRUTH is, that athlete is NOT FEELING PRESSURED. That athlete is relishing in the moment. That athlete is SUBCONSCIOUSLY CONFIDENT and KNOWS he/she IS PREPARED. That player has no EXPECTATIONS to win but only to give their best. Because this athlete is not feeling pressure, there is no lack of relaxation, no tensing up, and NO PANIC. The result will be to continue to compete with full physical capabilities and achieving personal ULTIMATE and/or BEST PERFORMANCES.

If an athlete competing in an individual sport is PRESSURED, they will stick out like a sore thumb, and they will not succeed, period.

When an athlete is competing in a team sport and is feeling the PRESSURE because they are not MENTALLY PREPARED, others can make up for that. You don't quite stick out as much, and as a team, you can still be successful. When an athlete feels PRESSURE, they stop being RELAXED; they STOP HAVING FUN. PLAYING a sport should always be FUN even though at times it can become INTENSE. INTENSITY and PERFORMING during INTENSE moments is part of the FUN! It would be tough to perform individually during INTENSE moments without this mental knowledge.

Here are some KEYS to having the ability to be relaxed, have fun, and enjoy the moment instead of having expectation:

- HAVE KNOWLEDGE OF YOURSELF AND YOUR SPORT.
- LEARN TO EMBRACE FAILURE.
- KNOW HOW TO TURN NEGATIVES INTO POSITIVES, AND LEARN FROM THE NEGATIVES and FAILURES. FACE FAILURE.
- CONFIDENCE—SUBCONSCIOUSLY AND CONSCIOUSLY.

NOTE: You may ask, "How do I gain confidence or have confidence?" This is the perfect answer:

CONFIDENCE IS KNOWING YOU ARE PREPARED.

Mental and physical preparation is a must. Remember, you are only as good as you are. Practice and preparation make you better. You don't get better during competition; you gain experience. Competition gives you your experience to learn from and shows you your potential and what you need to work on next. When you play and compete, just go out and give it your best; have FUN.

IF YOU DO WHAT YOU ALWAYS HAVE DONE, YOU WILL GET WHAT YOU HAVE ALWAYS GOTTEN

- KNOWLEDGE EQUALS NO FEAR. Knowing yourself and your sport strongly contributes to the feeling of no fear. If you have practiced and prepared to the best of your ability for a competition, there is NO FEAR. You KNOW you are prepared, and CONFIDENCE IS KNOWING YOU ARE PREPARED. You must believe this. This is the best answer for having confidence. You must convince yourself you are prepared and then go at it with NO EXPECTATION.
- KNOWLEDGE IS THE KEY, and TACTICS ARE THE POWER!

All this makes sense and sounds simple. Believe it or not, for some it is very difficult to buy into all this. There are many athletes who feel that having expectation is positive. Expectation is not positive. Being prepared and confident is positive. These two thought processes are different and will produce different results.

When observing various types of competitions, the team or individual that seems to know or acts like they know they are going to be successful are the ones with the least talent and tend to be unsuccessful. A great example of this is the singing competition *American Idol*. Over and over again, you will listen to a person talk about how great they are and that they are going to win. Imagine the expectations they have. In most cases, when you hear them sing, they can't hit a note. Amazing. Then you will listen to others say how they know this is a tough competition and they would be so happy just to make the first cut. They are humble and thankful just to have a chance to be in the competition. Usually, these people are the best singers with the most talent. Amazing. The humble ones have been around others who can also sing well and realize the competition and talent that is out there.

They have knowledge. The humble ones usually go on to Hollywood and get a try for the top twenty-four, and the most egotistical people are cut and act ridiculously angry. That anger comes from the huge expectations they had and then the reality of failure right in their face. Lack of knowledge and/or blatant ignorance really is at the forefront here. This same situation can be related to sports. Competition can humble you quickly.

When you choose an endeavor, you need to have and/or gain knowledge and experience at it. Use your references and honestly compare yourself to others. Try to get a true idea of where you are in the mix of things so you become aware of what you need to do to improve. Be realistic. Expectation, bragging, and acting overconfident doesn't get you anything but a hard fall.

PEOPLE MAY NOT BELIEVE WHAT YOU SAY, BUT THEY WILL ALWAYS BELIEVE WHAT YOU DO.

Keys for Expectation and Pressure

- NEVER EXPECT ANYTHING.
- DO NOT GIVE AWAY YOUR CONTROL.
- KNOW YOURSELF AND YOUR SPORT.
- BE READY TO GIVE YOUR BEST.
- THINK POSITIVE THOUGHTS OR DON'T THINK AT ALL.
- ACCEPT THAT YOU ARE ONLY AS GOOD AS YOU ARE.
- NO PRESSURE, NO PANIC.
- KNOW YOU ARE PREPARED. THIS CREATES CONFIDENCE.
- ACCEPT AND EMBRACE FAILURE, YOUR BEST TEACHER.
- HAVE FUN, ENJOY THE INTENSITY, ENJOY YOUR JOURNEY.

Success creates expectation and pressure. I believe it is tougher to deal with success than it is to deal with failure. The next sections will cover dealing with failure and success. Make your own judgments. Both success and failure are tricky to deal with.

SUCCESS AND FAILURE

What do you think would be easier to deal with, success or failure? This is an important question. The answer is, they are both very difficult to deal with. What is important is that you know how to deal with both. You might think, how can success be hard to deal with? Success is what everyone wants. When you are successful, things should become easier. It really is not easy to deal with success.

There are several keys to dealing with failure and mistakes. The most important one is realizing that everyone makes mistakes and everyone fails. Mistakes are part of competition and are one of the parts that you can learn the most from. It is smart to learn from your mistakes and failures. It is very common for athletes to allow failure and mistakes to hurt their confidence.

There are statements made by commentators or athletes about how they did this or that, and it hurt or helped their confidence. Example, a basketball player misses his/her first two shots, and the commentator remarks about how this will hurt the shooter's confidence. That same player makes their first shot in a game. A commentator will say, "It's good to see him/her get started early." That will help his/her confidence. These types of statements really make no sense. These types of statements prove how many people do not know what confidence is and how it is built.

Top-level athletes make statements that make no sense regarding confidence or the confidence that these athletes should have at all times. There are many athletes who do not know and/or understand what confidence and having confidence really is. They are confident, but they don't know why. If you don't know why you are confident, that makes it very easy to lose your confidence.

Athletes must know that if they are prepared, they are confident. If you know you have prepared and you are prepared, you are confident, period. The next thought for the prepared athlete is, "I AM ONLY AS GOOD AS I AM. GO PLAY AND TAKE WHAT I GET." Confidence is truly that simple. Start paying attention to what athletes say about their successes and failures. You can learn a lot about their mental game and compare it to yours and what you are learning. With the proper attitude, there is no pressure. You just go out and play and take what you get, period.

- WITHOUT MISTAKES AND FAILURES, THERE CANNOT BE PERFECTION OR SUCCESS.
- LEARN TO EMBRACE FAILURE. EMBRACE YOUR MISTAKES. These are your BEST TEACHERS. Yes, failure is disappointing, but that is what is supposed to fuel the fire inside of you. Failure and mistakes are what you learn from.

If you can learn to face your failures and analyze your mistakes, then they actually become a positive. Does anyone win every time? No! Success would mean nothing without failures. If you believe that you are simply in a process, your entire journey will become much more enjoyable. Competition is about learning to be the one or the team that makes the least mistakes so you are successful. After the competition, work on the mistakes.

Here is a way to think about success combined with failure. If a baseball player obtains a .400 batting average, that is considered very successful, but he/she is FAILING six out of ten times. If a basketball player is averaging 50% from the floor, that is extremely successful, but he/she is still FAILING five out of ten times. Those athletes are still working on improving those numbers. They are striving for perfection, and batting one thousand or shooting 100% is just not going to happen. No one has to be perfect to be very successful, even though that is what the athlete strives for. It may happen for one game, but not for a season. Failure and success go together.

Practice, drive, experience, analyzing, and much more go into becoming a great athlete. Most importantly, failure is about what you do with it in your mind. Failure is a motivator. Failure is positive. You must tell yourself that you are motivated by your failure, and you will improve because of it. Convince yourself you will learn from your failures.

So let's think about that athlete who has taken all the little steps and now is making big things happen. The athlete is becoming successful. Now the attention comes. Finally, this athlete is getting noticed. This can happen on a small scale like the school or city league level. It can also happen on a very large scale. A large-scale situation would be someone who has been chosen number one in a professional draft or signed a multimillion dollar contract.

The first-time highly successful athlete at the school level is likely going to feel the same types of things as the number one draft choice. The feelings of pressure and expectation start becoming a factor. This is exactly what makes success tough to deal with. Suddenly, the athlete is getting a lot of attention. This athlete has done well over and over again, with very consistent improvement. Now this athlete is being noticed everywhere they go. His/her picture is in the newspaper; more people are coming to watch. Lots of people are stopping this athlete just to say hello or get a picture or an autograph.

Now the expectation comes. Now this athlete is EXPECTED to keep performing well. The EXPECTATIONS he/she now has and the expectations others have can become devastating if not handled mentally correctly by the athlete. When this athlete begins to realize that people expect great things, the pressure can start creeping in. Now the athlete may begin to press himself or herself, attempting to do even more than they are capable of. Then the mistakes come, the failure, and the disappointment. Once this happens, the athlete has not only disappointed himself or herself, that athlete has let down a whole lot of other people. Now the athlete is asked about what happened. A lot of the comments are now not so positive. Many times, the situation can roll downhill from this point. There is now more pressure to perform. The athlete can become very mentally involved with going out and PROVING he/she can do it again instead of just continuing with their plan and their journey. When success comes, the athlete must be mentally strong in order to deal with it properly. The athlete must know success and failure will come and go.

See how the pattern can develop. If you do not know how to handle success, when it comes, you could get in deep trouble fast. A great example of this is a young woman golfer who got a huge monetary endorsement. She skipped the college experience. She then played too much, against to many greater opponents without success, then came an injury. She had lots of expectation around her and likely felt a lot of pressure. This player got in deep trouble.

Too much pressure caused her to play far from 100% of her capabilities. Then the physical failure crept into the body, then into the mind, and that pretty much crippled the player. This player needs to slow down, get physically and mentally healed, and slowly get back into competition. This player has a long way to go. She is young, so she has time on her side. Hopefully, she has the right people with the right knowledge to get her back to where she was mentally, so she has the opportunity to reach her highest potential. This is one reason success can be tougher to deal with than failure. Usually, what goes up must come down. If you go up too fast without the proper mental preparation, the fall could be a hard one.

Since this was first written, this particular player has since won her first LPGA tournament in November of 2009. It was the final tournament of her rookie season. Awesome!

Success is a wonderful thing, and it is very necessary to pay a price for it. There was a professional bowler who won the first pro tournament she entered. It took her more than six years to win again. That is all mental, too much, too soon, too fast. Too much expectation and pressure created too early in a career can really damage the process of becoming successful and consistently successful. She absolutely did not know how to handle the instant success. It is fun to get attention and be successful, but success can lead to failure waiting right around the corner. Dealing with success can be tough and tricky. You will learn how to succeed, and you need to know how to deal with the success. This is very important.

Experience is something you cannot learn, buy, or teach. We all have to get experience at everything in order to learn how to deal with what we are doing. It is all about making the most of your precious experiences, whether they are good or bad ones.

An important factor to remember is that success only shows you your potential for future endeavors. The idea of success and fame is a pleasing idea in just about anyone's mind. I have given only a couple of examples of what can happen when someone has too much success too soon and doesn't know how to handle it. There are lots and lots of people who have become rich, famous, and successful, then turned around and lost everything.

There is one glaring example in sports of a very famous heavyweight boxer. His whole situation is very sad. He not only had no idea how to deal with success, he didn't know who to trust, and he didn't really know how to handle life very well. This athlete truly needed a MENTOR. He obviously wasn't willing to listen to good influences around him, and/or there just were never good influences around him. I believe some people used his talent for their own personal gain and really did not care about him at all. That is a very sad situation, and these situations happen all the time, all over the planet. Become educated enough that you cannot be taken advantage of.

Here is some more food for thought: I have heard there are a lot of people who have won the lotto and are now flat broke. Again, people not knowing how to deal with having lots of money, which often comes with lots of success. The lotto is just luck, but apparently, there are a lot of people who don't know how to deal with being rich. When success comes, I do hope you know who your true friends are. When a person becomes successful, they really have a lot more "friends" all of a sudden. A prime example of this was following the 2008 Summer Olympics when Michael Phelps clearly stated during a post-Olympic interview that over the last few years, he truly found out who his friends are. It is important for everyone to know who their friends really are. This really is another part of dealing with big success. It is important to know who really loves and cares about you.

KEYS FOR DEALING WITH FAILURE

1. Know that everyone fails and makes mistakes.
2. Analyze your failures and mistakes, grab them by the throat, and face them.
3. Make a plan to limit and/or eliminate the mistakes and/or failures.
4. Allow yourself to learn from your mistakes and failures. They are your best teachers.
5. Make failure positive. Keys 1 through 4 help you to do this.

ALWAYS REMEMBER AND NEVER FORGET

1. Success is not about winning but about making fewer mistakes than your opponent.
2. Failure is the fuel that stokes the fire of success.
3. Without failure, there cannot be success.

Sounds simple, and if it were easy, everybody would handle failure and success well.

KEYS FOR DEALING WITH SUCCESS

1. Know that success only shows you your potential for future endeavors.
2. Little steps make big things happen. Keep taking little steps.
3. Be gracious, humble, and thankful. This is very important.
4. Confidence is knowing you are prepared. Continue with your preparation and planning.
5. Remember, there is always someone out there working harder than you are. Respect others. Work hard.
6. No team or individual remains on top for long. Your competition is right on your back.
7. Enjoy your process. It will go up and down; you want to keep that process consistent.
8. Knowledge equals no fear. Know yourself and your game.
9. Do not take success for granted. Failure can be just around the corner.
10. Enjoy the moment. Enjoy your journey, and remember, it is just a journey.

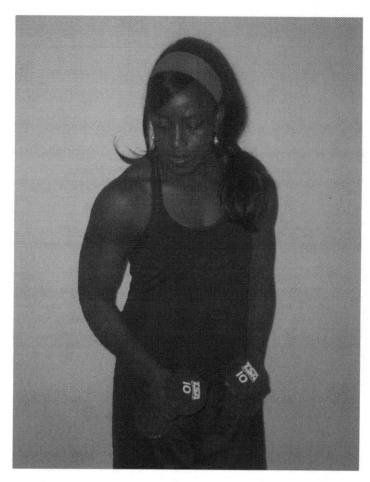

Ruthie looks dissatisfied as if she has failed.

Ruthie is looking strong, successful and satisfied. Ruthie has been retired from professional basketball about 7 years and she still exercises and stays in great shape. Pride is a key to sport and life success.

KEYS FOR REACHING YOUR HIGHEST POTENTIAL

Without this knowledge, reaching your full potential and becoming a very successful athlete or professional athlete is nearly impossible. Consciously having this knowledge is much better than having it subconsciously and not being able to put it into words. Successful athletes live by many or all these keys and may not even know it or be able to put it into words. Following the lists of keys and key phrases are an explanation or expansion of the keys.

GIVING YOUR BEST

HONOR, PRIDE, INTEGRITY, HONESTY, EGO, HEART, PASSION

SELF-RESPONSIBILITY, PERSONAL CHOICES

SELF-ESTEEM

SETTING GOALS

HARD-WORK WORK ETHIC, SELF-MOTIVATION

PHYSICAL PRACTICE

TEACHING FEEL, LEARNING FEEL

MENTAL PRACTICE

THE MENTAL GAME

FEAR

SUBCONSCIOUS MIND VERSUS CONSCIOUS MIND

PATIENCE AND DISCIPLINE

EXPECTATION AND PRESSURE

FAILURE AND SUCCESS

KNOWLEDGE

CONFIDENCE

ALWAYS ENJOY THE JOURNEY

It takes a team to succeed. Friends, coaches, mentors and teammates are a part of individual success.

Jared is in a triple threat position. Hard work, practice, focus, dedication and giving your best are important keys. Jared works on his basketball game 25 to 30 hours per week. He plays professional basketball in Italy and his dream and goal is to play in the NBA.

KEY PHRASES

As an athlete and a person, if you are willing to compete and live by these phrases, they can greatly assist you in becoming a better athlete and reaching your highest potential. These are positive affirmations to assist you physically and mentally. Your journey will become much more enjoyable and worthwhile as you begin to make these affirmations part of you.

IF YOU FAIL TO PLAN, YOU PLAN TO FAIL.

CONFIDENCE IS KNOWING YOU ARE PREPARED.

KNOWLEDGE EQUALS NO FEAR.

YOU CAN'T BUY EXPERIENCE, AND YOU CAN'T LEARN IT.

KNOWLEDGE IS THE KEY; TACTICS ARE THE POWER.

WHEN THE STUDENT IS READY, THE TEACHER WILL COME.

A FRIEND TELLS YOU WHAT YOU NEED TO HEAR,
NOT WHAT YOU WANT TO HEAR.

LITTLE THINGS MAKE BIG THINGS HAPPEN.

COMPETITION IS NOT A VIDEO GAME—IT IS REAL.
It takes time and hard work to make big and good things happen.

GOOD LUCK IS PREDICATED ON HARD WORK.

LEARN HOW TO DO ONE THING TO THE VERY BEST OF YOUR ABILITY.
Then you will know how to become accomplished at anything.

YOU CAN SPEND TIME LOOKING FOR SOMETHING OR NOTHING.
You can spend your time doing and earning something for yourself. Earn something for yourself and you gain pride. You will feel much better about what you have acquired.

COACHES/TEACHERS WILL NOT MAKE YOU GOOD AT ANYTHING.
You make yourself good by working hard at what you do on your own time. Coaches/teachers will guide you and help you to improve and become successful.

IF YOU DO WHAT YOU HAVE ALWAYS DONE, YOU WILL GET WHAT YOU HAVE ALWAYS GOTTEN.

THERE IS NO SUCH THING AS INSTINCT.
IT IS REALLY LEARNED BEHAVIOR.

SUCCESS ONLY SHOWS YOU YOUR POTENTIAL.
YOU LEARN MORE FROM YOUR FAILURES.
FACE FAILURE—GRAB IT BY THE THROAT, ANALYZE IT,
AND LEARN FROM IT.

EMBRACE FAILURE FOR IT IS YOUR FRIEND, AS IT IS YOUR BEST TEACHER CONCERNING FUTURE SUCCESSES.

FAILURE IS THE FUEL THAT STOKES THE FIRES OF SUCCESS.

SUCCESS IS NOT A DESTINATION BUT MERELY A JOURNEY.

SUCCESS IS NOT ABOUT WINNING BUT SIMPLY ABOUT FAILING LESS THAN YOUR COMPETITION.

SOME SUCCEED BECAUSE THEY ARE DESTINED. MOST SUCCEED BECAUSE THEY ARE DETERMINED.

QUITTING IS THE EASIEST THING TO DO
BECAUSE IT REQUIRES NO TALENT.

IF IT WERE EASY, EVERYBODY WOULD BE DOING IT.

BE DETERMINED AND KEEP GOING.
THE MOST TALENTED MAY JUST NOT WIN.

PERSEVERANCE—BE WILLING TO WORK HARD.
THERE ARE HUGE PAYOFFS FOR PREPARATION AND HARD WORK.

ALWAYS ENJOY YOUR JOURNEY.

You may want to write up a personal list of keys for yourself to compete and live by. This will help to keep you on a positive path and achieve your goals. Here are some examples:

1. ALWAYS GIVE YOUR BEST.
2. BE HONEST.
3. COMPETE WITH HONOR AND PRIDE.
4. ALWAYS HOLD ON TO YOUR INTEGRITY.
5. RESPECT YOURSELF, YOUR STUDENTS, YOUR PEERS, YOUR COMPETITION, YOUR PARENTS, AND YOUR TEACHERS.
6. PRACTICE AND WORK ON THE THINGS YOU CANNOT DO WELL.
7. HAVE A PLAN. SET GOALS FOR YOURSELF.
8. GIVE BACK.
9. BE A GOOD ROLE MODEL.
10. DO NOT CHEAT. IF YOU CHEAT AND WIN, YOU DID NOT WIN!
11. FAILURE IS OK. ACCEPT FAILURE AS ONE OF YOUR TEACHERS.
12. GIVE YOUR BEST AT PRACTICE AND BE ON TIME.

These are ten phrases that would be great for young children to be aware of. How you grew up, the environment you grew up in, the people and friends around that you grew up with do have a huge impact on what and who you become as a person and an athlete. If you have not checked into your past to learn to know yourself, it would be a great thing for you to do. You just may learn what makes you tick, why you want to become great at something. Knowing yourself is a great motivator.

TEN AFFIRMATIONS FOR YOUNG CHILDREN

Teasing or bullying is very negative.
This can cause a lifetime of pain for the recipient.

Ask questions; do not be afraid or hesitant to ask questions.

Get involved with positive groups and activities.

Remember, no one can do everything, but everyone can do something.

Judging others is negative. You have not walked in their shoes.

Criticizing others is negative. You have not walked in their shoes.

Be supportive. Include everyone you can.

Be aware of how YOU FEEL. Trust yourself and your guts.

Be careful about whom you trust, and trust no strangers.

If someone is hurting you physically or hurting your feelings
and/or you feel scared, tell someone you trust.

Life time memories and relationships are built which serve as a great reward for competing. Ruthie, Jared and Damond are lifetime friends because of basketball.

Feelings of satisfaction, confidence, high self-esteem and no regrets are rewards for living by the keys to success. Ruthie and Shirley have great sport resumes'. Ruthie's resume is highlighted with 2 OLYMPIC GOLD MEDALS and Shirley has 1 Regional Professional Bowling Title.

EXPANSION OF KEYS

GIVING YOUR BEST is one of the most important factors of excelling in athletics and life. If you always give your best and never cheat, you can always feel good about yourself and what you do. Giving your best promotes feeling high self-esteem. When you always give your best, you are automatically a winner.

Giving your best doesn't mean wiping yourself out at everything you do. When you are doing something, you focus on that task and give it your best effort. Make the most of the time you are spending. It really makes no difference if you are at work, at practice, doing yard work, or playing a board game. Enjoy what you are doing and give it your best. Make it a habit with everything you do, and you will shine as an athlete, student, employee, and as a person.

Practice makes your game what it is. The competition only shows you your potential and what you need to practice on. At a team practice, everyone involved will appreciate you giving your best. It will set an excellent example for everyone. If you are fortunate enough to be able to take private lessons, which can be expensive, do your best at your lessons. Pay attention and take notes. If you pay for lessons, it is a great idea to write down what you learn. You will always have that information to refer back to. At times, like when you are in a slump, you can look back on notes and find something to help you.

The following is an example of how an individual could make the best of a practice session: You are a basketball player going out on your own to practice shooting the ball. First, have a plan. Know how many shots you are going to take and from what spots. FOCUS on what you are doing, and make every shot important in your mind. Don't waste shots. Pay attention to form, what feels good and balanced. Start out close to the basket and work your way out. Keep track of the spots you shoot from, makes, and misses. Note them on paper. Then you KNOW what you have done, you KNOW your shooting percentage, and you can track your improvement as you practice these shots more.

This is a small example of giving your best at a practice session. Only you know what giving your best is. By following a plan, this allows you to know you have given a good effort to improve your game. This builds confidence. We all know when we are lax in our efforts. We can always do more and work harder at anything we do. The key really is PAYING ATTENTION to what we are doing at that moment. FOCUS on what you are doing and don't waste time. That is much of what giving your best is about.

Another example would be, if you decide to go on a twenty-minute jog/run every day, as the days go on, that run will get easier for you. Noting the distance you go will show your improvement. If you choose to focus on increasing the distance every run, you will, most likely, increase it every time for many days. At some point, your distance will plateau. It will start to be hard to increase the distance you run in twenty minutes. At that point, you add time to your run, and so on.

THE MORE WE DO, THE MORE WE CAN DO.
IF YOU DO WHAT YOU HAVE ALWAYS DONE,
YOU WILL GET WHAT YOU HAVE ALWAYS GOTTEN.

These examples are ideas and/or ways to be giving it your best. You have a goal for your start, and you set a higher goal each time for yourself. You set up a reasonable goal for yourself that is comfortable for you and improve upon that starting goal each time you do that task. Everybody is different on how hard he/she can work and how much he/she can do. Use your best judgment on giving it your best. The consistency is what builds your abilities. The planning and seeing your improvement and results is what builds your confidence. In a sense, you are training your subconscious mind with good habits. This helps your body to respond appropriately when you want it to.

GIVING YOUR BEST during an actual competition would be the following: You have already practiced and prepared for a competition. Practice is where the work is. Now it is time to enjoy your work. You get to go out and see how good you are. You must know in your mind before the competition that you are only as good as you are, whatever that may be. You relax, focus on the moment, and play your game. NO WHINING! You play with your head up, note your mistakes subconsciously, and keep playing. When the competition is over, whether you win or lose, you analyze your personal mistakes so you know what to work on. Then it is on to the next practice.

The most important thing for you to feel when you come away from a competition is that you gave it your best effort. Knowing you are only as good as you are will help you to feel much less pressure at game time. Just go out and do your thing when competing. Don't have expectations of yourself. If you feel you gave your best at the end, then you are a WINNER no matter what the result.

In summary, always giving your best is one of the most important keys to reaching your highest potential. Giving your best is an ATTITUDE. I love what Charles Swindoll wrote about attitude:

ATTITUDE

The longer I live, the more I realize the impact of attitude on life.

ATTITUDE, to me, is more important than facts.
It is more important than the past, than education,
than money, than circumstances, than failures,
than successes, than what other people think or
say or do. It is more important than appearance,
giftedness, or skill. It will make or break a
company . . . a church . . . a home.
The remarkable thing is we have a choice every day
regarding the attitude we will embrace for that day.
We cannot change the inevitable. The only thing
we can do is play on the one string we have,
and that is our ATTITUDE . . .
I am convinced that life is 10% what happens to me
and 90% how I react to it.
and so it is with you . . .
We are in charge of our ATTITUDE.

(CHARLES SWINDOLL)

HONOR, PRIDE, INTEGRITY, HONESTY, EGO, HEART

HONOR AND PRIDE: Compete with honor and pride. Respect your sport, peers, teachers, and yourself. If a person is constantly knocking their competition or peers, then what are they really saying about themselves? What are they the best of? Be a good role model. People are watching, and children are watching and learning from you. Set a good example.

Honor is a big issue. The sport of golf really is a good example of a sport of honor. When you are playing, it is very easy to cheat. Always write down how many shots it really took to get the ball in the hole. How can you know of your improvement and how good you are if you do not count every shot? It is a dishonorable thing to "get away" with something when you could have called it on yourself. If you do this and succeed, you really did not succeed.

Honor coincides with pride. You should always be proud of yourself and your sport. Set a good example by looking and acting appropriately. We have all seen and heard about many different situations that professional athletes get involved in that give them and their sport a bad name. Taking pride in you and your sport means that you should look and act appropriately at all times. DO NOT DO ANYTHING THAT YOU WOULD NOT WANT IN THE NEWSPAPER.

INTEGRITY: Adherence to a code or standard of values. The quality or condition of being undivided is COMPLETENESS. Being honest with yourself, your competition, and others proves integrity. Integrity is about following rules and procedures. Integrity could mean something like calling a penalty on yourself in a golf game or calling a foul on yourself when playing a pickup game of basketball. Competition has rules for a reason. People do break and push the rules. Coaches and competitors that truly love competition play fair. They do not humiliate a weaker opponent. Always compete with integrity.

HONESTY is an important subject. DO NOT CHEAT AT ANYTHING YOU DO. IF YOU DO AND YOU WIN, YOU DID NOT WIN. It is amazing that someone can cheat, win, and then come and shake your hand with a straight face. It is so wrong! No one gets to know who the true winner is. It is a shameful situation, and it occurs in far too many places in sports.

It is often said that everybody lies. That is probably true. The most important thing about being honest is being honest with you. You are the best one to know the truth about you. Being honest is the best and easiest path to good communication.

Remember, the true friend will TELL YOU WHAT YOU NEED TO HEAR, NOT WHAT YOU WANT TO HEAR.

Being honest with others is very important. If you are consistently honest, you usually have nothing to hide. If you don't lie, you don't have to worry about lying again to cover up a previous lie. Being consistently honest keeps life much simpler. Lying to important people in your life is really serious. It is just not worth it. You will find if you really focus on being honest, your life in general will remain much simpler. Usually, people are much happier just hearing the truth and dealing with it, no matter how bad the truth may be. By being honest, things can be handled much more correctly and efficiently. A very honest person would have a very difficult time cheating. Cheating at any competition is horrific.

EGO: It is very important to have a strong mind when you are a competitor. As you improve, it is also important to keep your head between your ears. Most people do not appreciate a cocky athlete. When an athlete starts acting and talking like he/she is better than everyone else, they become annoying. No one stays on top for long. You can be humbled very quickly in athletics. If you are a cocky athlete, you will not have too many admirers, and when you do fall, fail, and/or become humiliated, you will be hard-pressed to find any help. Most of us are aware of the cocky professional athletes. They are not usually fan favorites, and they really set a poor example for young athletes.

The way you keep your head between your ears is this: Don't ever forget where you came from and how you got where you are. Do not forget those who helped you along the way. Do not forget that there is always someone right on your butt, and when you let up, they will be taking your spot. Always be thankful for your health, and know one injury could make everything change. Respect your competition, and respect all the people that give you support. Without the supporters, you would be nothing. Never forget you are only one tiny speck on this planet, and in the big picture, your journey is mostly important to you. Be humble and stay humble. Keep your journey positive.

HEART: This is an athlete that will never say die. It doesn't matter how talented they are. They are just a special sort of athlete who keeps going and giving it everything they have to give. This may be a star or a role player, but not every player has HEART. A great movie to watch about a person who has a huge heart is RUDY. He loved the game of football, and he kept playing no matter what circumstances came his way. Having heart is a gift. Fans love athletes and teams with heart.

Professional athletes who play as if their heart is bigger than the building they are in like Jon Barry (NBA) and Yolanda Griffith (WNBA) are big fan favorites. Players like this are sports heroes. A player can develop the have-heart attitude by always giving their best.

PASSION: Loving to win and hating to lose is passion. This feeling develops a passion for doing everything it takes to succeed. Failing keeps the passion for success strong. Being passionate about competition is very positive and a gift. When you compete, you want to be in the ZONE. Nothing else is there, just you and what you are doing. The passion is doing it. Your entire mind and body are into it. Money cannot buy this feeling. When you can be involved in what you are passionate about, life is very good. When you can achieve your goals involving what you are passionate about, it is a priceless feeling.

Whatever it is that lights the fire within you is what you need to use for yourself to be passionate. It could be that you simply want to prove yourself to others for whatever personal reasons you have. If that is what motivates you, that is great. Being passionate about proving yourself can be very motivating and positive.

If you are doing what you love, the PASSION is there. Self-motivation and determination to reach your goals and highest potential has a lot to do with passion.

PASSION IS ABOUT ALWAYS GIVING YOUR BEST

SELF-RESPONSIBILITY AND PERSONAL CHOICES: What you do is mostly up to you. As an athlete and person, you should be well aware that self-responsibility and personal choices are an extremely important part of success.

Everybody wants attention. In most cases, we do not get attention for being good. We always get lots of attention when we are bad. Therefore, many people growing up make bad decisions because they get attention.

Try to look at it this way: if no one is paying much attention to me, I must be doing well. It is really true too. This is something most learn way later in life. IT IS GOOD IF YOU ARE NOT GETTING MUCH ATTENTION BECAUSE THAT MEANS YOU ARE DOING GOOD THINGS. Then, all those good little steps make really good things happen and you get your attention. Attention like graduating at or near the top or being on a winning team or making a spectacular play. The attention will and does come if you are good; it just takes a lot more time.

When you are bad, you get immediate attention. Negative attention is no fun; positive attention is awesome. Hold out for the positive attention. There can be challenges every day for you while growing up. You must be strong and trust yourself and make good and positive choices for yourself. For the most part, the better and smarter your choices, the easier your life will be. IT TRULY IS UP TO YOU HOW LIFE GOES FOR YOU. Your parents, teachers, and coaches are only guides. YOU HAVE TO LIVE WITH THE CHOICES YOU MAKE. You are the one who will have to live with and pay for the consequences of poor choices.

At a very young age, we began making choices. The more good information and guidance you are given the better choices you make for yourself. By the time we reach the age of about ten or eleven, we have lots of choices and decisions to make every day. As we grow older, the choices become more important and more difficult. If you are self-responsible and make good choices, you will go much further than others at a much faster rate.

It is important to realize at a young age that the choices you make do affect your life. School presents students with choices every single day. The peer pressures can be great. It is important to be strong, trust yourself, make good decisions, and do not get yourself into bad situations. When you are able to establish a good foundation for making good and positive choices for yourself, then in turn, good and positive results will occur.

Bottom line, we all know the difference between right and wrong. We know if we cheat or play by the rules. Playing by the rules does not mean just at a sport. This means school rules, parent's rules, and life rules. It is very important to understand that cheating at anything does not do anyone any good and making wrong decisions doesn't usually create positive results either. THE CHOICES ARE YOURS, and you have to live with the choices and pay the consequences of your choices.

In summary, self-responsibility and positive personal choices are big keys to becoming successful. It is really up to you.

SELF-ESTEEM: This is about how good you feel about yourself. Working hard, giving your best, having pride, and making failure positive are great keys to having high self-esteem. Do not believe negative comments made to you or about you. If you do, you are giving those people control of your feelings. Believe in yourself in a positive way. Personal care and how you appear are other factors of feeling higher self-esteem. If you look good on the outside, it helps you to feel better about yourself on the inside.

When self-esteem is damaged, it can be devastating to an individual. All athletes should be encouraged equally. If you happen to be on a team where certain players are favored, it is not a good situation. The important thing for you is to not let that hurt you. Know yourself, stay strong, and next time, you will hopefully be in a better situation. Everyone on a team should be encouraged equally, and equal attention should be given to the positives and negatives concerning every player. Criticism among players and criticism from parents should not be allowed during practices or games. Positive comments should be strongly encouraged. This builds everyone's self-esteem and confidence. If you are in a situation like this, you are on a good team with a good leader.

In summary, having high self-esteem is a must. Most importantly, do not let anyone lower your self-esteem. Believe in yourself and stay positive. Ignore the negative comments.

SETTING GOALS: Having goals is mandatory. If you do not have goals, you are not alive. It is important to set reasonable goals for yourself. Keep in mind that there are many people who simply have the goal of finding food and a place to sleep. Always respect life, and be thankful if you are in a place in your life where you can set some good and positive goals. There are daily, weekly, monthly, yearly, and lifetime goals to think about.

Do not waste time. Make a list and have a plan for the day. Go to sleep at night feeling that you accomplished something. Achieving goals is not easy. Always remember, IF YOU FAIL TO PLAN, YOU PLAN TO FAIL.

Setting goals for your personal achievements is very positive. With goals in mind, you will tend to plan individual practice and set up goals for that session. It is a good idea to plan when you will be at school or work, when you will do your homework, when you will practice, and when you will have your rest and relaxation time. Athletes with very full schedules who practice and go to school may even have their sleep and shower time scheduled. It is a good idea to have daily, weekly, monthly, and yearly goals. Setting goals is an important key for improvement.

HARD-WORK WORK ETHIC: Life is not a video game. It is real. All of us today see things happen so fast—in the movies, on TV, in video games, and on the Internet. This can really make people think things are easy. No one gets good at anything without practice and hard work. Hard work comes with huge payoffs. Hard work raises self-esteem. When you earn something because you put in the work to earn it, it means much more to you. You will feel a sense of pride that is like no other.

The hard-work work ethic comes from SELF-MOTIVATION. Really, hard work and self-motivation go hand in hand. Coaches can push you and motivate you during your time together, but you must motivate and push yourself outside of those lessons and practice sessions. The high achiever is SELF-MOTIVATED. The high achiever works hard outside of team practices or lessons. As an example, when coaches give you suggestions of things to work on, they are serious. They know that just practices and lessons alone will not allow you to reach your highest potential. You have to put in extra work to reach your full potential. The athlete that takes on their coach's suggestions and uses them will usually be the highest achievers on the team, no matter what natural talent they were given. Again, hard work pays big, and being a hard worker comes from within you.

For athletes, the hard work is done at practice time and between practices. When the written plan is complete, it is time for the physical hard work. It is important to focus during your practice time and give everything a good effort. Your practice time and hard work during that time is the basis for your future endeavors, failures, and/or successes as a team and as an individual. Players who put in the work always get payoffs for the extra practice. The more you do, the more you can do.

PHYSICAL PRACTICE: Feel and injury are covered in the "Physical Practice" chapter.

MENTAL PRACTICE/GAME: The subconscious versus the conscious mind, patience, discipline, and fear are covered in the "Mental Practice" chapter.

EXPECTATION AND PRESSURE are covered in the chapter with the same title.

FAILURE AND SUCCESS are covered in the chapter with the same title.

KNOWLEDGE: Having knowledge about what you are doing is obviously extremely important. You gain knowledge of yourself as you go through your journey of life and competition. Know your strengths and weaknesses. You must know what causes your adrenaline to flow and/or to get out of control. Learn how to pace yourself. Know what makes you angry or frustrated, and know how to deal with that anger or frustration and control it. Know your plan and stick to your plan. Know how to deal with failure, success, expectation, and pressure. You learn much of this through studying, practice, competition, lessons, and experience. In short, KNOWLEDGE EQUALS NO FEAR.

CONFIDENCE: CONFIDENCE IS KNOWING YOU ARE PREPARED, PERIOD.

Don't ask yourself anymore why you are not confident. Prepare yourself to the best of your ability, and go compete. You are only who you are. You are only as good as you are. You can only do what you can do. So do what you can do and go give your best at your competition. You are as prepared as you can be. If you are scared to death or dread your competition, it is time to ask questions, get a teacher, get some lessons, practice more—whatever it takes for you to be and feel prepared. If you have given your best to prepare and you love what you are about to do, YOU ARE PREPARED. GO COMPETE WITH CONFIDENCE. Do not worry about anyone or anything else. JUST GO DO YOUR THING! Take what you get and MOVE ON! Being confident is truly this simple.

ENJOY THE JOURNEY: If you are not enjoying what you are doing, you are already in trouble. Life and competition are like a wave, going up and down and up and down. The whole idea about going through your journey is that the ups are not too up and the downs are not too down. Too up and too down are both negative. You may think, why wouldn't I want to be up all the time? You do want to be up all the time, but the problem is that it's basically impossible. If you were up all the time, then *up* really wouldn't exist. No one wins every time; no one is happy every moment.

This information is not to help you win every time. It is so that you feel like a winner all the time. This is to help you reach your highest potential and to give you some ideas on how to deal with failure and how to look at failure as positive. This information is about learning how to go through your journey smoothly. An up is a big success, and it should always feel great. A low is a failure of some sort, and it never feels that good. You must learn to enjoy the win for what it is. Know that it has shown you something about your potential, and know to keep your ego intact. Don't put too much weight on success, or things can get out of hand quickly.

Here is an example of too much good and too much bad during an athletic journey: During 2007, a professional quarterback was arrested. This story was known of nationally. His crimes involved animals. He is going to spend some time in jail. He has been suspended from being part of his team. It was said that he grew up in not such a good environment (that is the too-much-bad part), then he became very successful. He signed a 130-million-dollar ten-year contract. Now he is going to jail. This is a really good example of too much bad and too much good, and someone not knowing how to deal with either. You can see very clearly that big success can turn into a huge negative very quickly if the success is not handled appropriately.

Learn to look at failure with realism. Know you can learn from it. Look at the failure and let it help you do better the next time. This way, you don't get too high or too low. This is a great help for you to always enjoying your journey. It is just a journey. We all get to go through a life journey, and fortunate people get to experience the athletic journey. An athletic journey is fun and priceless. Most athletes would not trade their athletic journey for anything.

Each and every one of these keys is important for you to know about and learn to make a part of your life and sports in order to reach your highest potential. Incorporate these keys as part of your life. These keys will assist you in being more balanced and happy. Using the methods provided should assist you in becoming a very satisfied competitor.

ALWAYS ENJOY YOUR JOURNEY.

STORIES FROM ATHLETES

RUTHIE BOLTON:
Professional basketball player/
WNBA TWO-TIME OLYMPIC GOLD MEDALIST,
WNBA HALL OF FAME

Ruthie, nicknamed Mighty Ruthie by WNBA fans, is one of the finest examples of a complete athlete and great person who exists on our planet, in my humble opinion. Her work ethic is very strong. During her career, she was one of the fittest athletes ever. She is also a loving and giving person who cares very much about what is around her.

The environment that a child was raised in has much to do with the child growing into a happy adult and reaching their fullest potential. Ruthie was raised in an excellent environment, and this was a big help in her reaching her potential.

I was honored and lucky to be able to connect with Ruthie. I am very thankful that she was willing to write a story for this book. I was also fortunate to watch her play for the Sacramento Monarchs for all her eight seasons there and to attend clinics that she was a part of, which helped make me a better youth coach and teacher. Please enjoy the short story of her fine journey of life as a Bolton and her basketball experience. Everyone can learn something from Ruthie.

RICHARD BATTLES:
Completed half triathlon at age fifty-eight after twelve months of training—amazing.

Richard weighed 223 pounds in February of 2003 when he purchased a bike and trained seriously from July 2004 to July 2005, and began the competition at 173 pounds at age fifty-eight. I am grateful he was willing to write a short story for this book. It is very inspirational. This is proof that it is never too late to succeed if you put your mind to it.

Proudly, Richard is my brother, ten years older than me. I was fortunate to help out here and there during his training. I was with him the first time he swam in open water. He said he was scared to death and barely finished that first swim. I was there for his start in the Russian River and at the finish line in Santa Rosa when he came across it. It was an overwhelming and inspirational experience. On that day, he became one of my sports heroes. He was always a great brother, and I love him very much. I am so proud of him.

I wish everyone could read this story. Richard really achieved something great!

Currently Ruthie does motivational speaking especially for the youth. She still lives by all the keys, is a very hard worker and stays in great shape as you can see.

Ruthie's 2 Olympic Gold Medals
are two of her proudest achievements as an athlete.

RUTHIE'S STORY

On May 25, 1967, I was the sixteenth born of twenty children in McLain, Mississippi. I was blessed to be a part of such a large family. My family was truly a part of me becoming successful as an athlete. We were always competing at something. By constantly seeing who could jump a creek the most times, climb a hill the fastest, or throw a rock the farthest, I got natural athletic training and developed a very competitive mind.

Discipline, structure, and positive life principles were very important to my father. He taught us how to adjust to the many things that happen in life. He stressed the importance of having a positive attitude. My father made sure we understood that there was always a lesson to be learned from any experience, be it negative or positive. I really had my own mentor at home, and he taught me well.

My mother was very positive. She made sure we were loved and given lots of attention. Being healthy and active and eating properly were high priorities on Mom's list. She always stressed the importance of eating vegetables, taking vitamins, and getting proper rest.

I was truly blessed to have such great parents, brothers, and sisters. This was my strong foundation to build on for my own personal success. I didn't realize this then, but I know it now.

I participated in several sports and games during my youth. My family played pickup basketball games often. We had two full teams with substitutes just from the family members. My first organized basketball game was in junior high school. I also participated in track as a relay sprinter.

While in junior high, ninth grade, I decided I wanted to play basketball in college. My older sister was being recruited as a tenth grader, and I became inspired by her. I began working harder to perfect my game outside of practice. I went on to play at McLain High School, following my older sister.

Auburn University was locking in on a scholarship for my sister by her senior year. There were no colleges pursuing me, and I considered quitting basketball then. My father told me he believed I could get that college scholarship, and that gave me a big incentive to keep going. Dad believed in me, and he made it simple. He said, "Life will throw you curves. You have no control over what people think. But you have your attitude, and you have a choice." So I went for it and continued to work hard on my game.

While dealing with Auburn University and my older sister's scholarship, my father made an agreement with the school. He proposed that if my older sister attended Auburn, they would give me a scholarship there the following season. Auburn agreed.

During my senior year, no colleges were recruiting me. Finally, Auburn called, and I took the bus trip there. It was upsetting to hear that they had called me there to tell me they didn't want me. But they told me they would keep their word to my father, and I was given a basketball scholarship to Auburn University. Wow! It was really time to get to work.

At Auburn, the practices were at least two hours and then another hour of weight training, five days a week. I worked up to bench-pressing about 200 pounds. I think my best bench press ever was about 280 pounds. Fortunately, because of my parents, I was disciplined and was aware of having a proper diet, getting good rest, and scheduling my time. My major was physiology, so I had a very full and strict schedule. It was very important to be scheduled and to value every minute each day.

Looking back on all this, it is hard for me to believe that I started my first year at Auburn. I was mostly a defensive player and passer. Great basketball does begin with defense. Our coach had us visualize the game and how it would be played as part of our game preparation. I always visualized the plays and making perfect passes before our games. This method really worked. Many of the things I visualized did happen.

The team's hard work paid off. My freshman year, we won the section title, and we did that three seasons of the four that I was there. We got close to the final four on my first year. During my junior and senior seasons, we made it to the final four. We did not make it to the championship game in '93 or '94. These were two of the most disappointing experiences of my basketball career. Making it that far twice but not going all the way was painful. Auburn was a great experience for me. After my four seasons there, I was second all the time in assists for the school, but that did not help the pain of not making it to the championship game two seasons in a row. I had to find a way to get the pain to go away. I began to think about the Olympic team.

There were fifty players invited to the tryout, and about one hundred players paid their own way to try out. I was not one of the invited fifty players. I had heard, if you were not in that group, you had very little chance to make the team. I decided to pay my way and try out for the team.

During the two-week tryouts, there were daily cuts. My name kept appearing on the list. The final day, we were told there would be twenty-five names on the next list, and if your name was there, you made the team. It was a big moment for me when I slowly looked at the list and saw my name. I had beaten the odds and made the team. It was almost unbelievable to me.

During my first season, I was on the secondary squad. Around this time, I was encouraged by Tara VanDerveer to start shooting. She told me I had good potential for being a scoring player. I began practicing on my three-point shooting and all other shots many hours per week outside of team practice.

We played a season in England, and we were undefeated. For that season, I was voted Player of the Year. I was so thankful and humbled being among such great players. When I think about how I was going to quit when I was younger and then to achieve this prestigious award, it amazed me. Developing the never-give-up attitude does have payoffs.

For 1996, I was invited to the tryouts and remained a part of TEAM USA for many years. The team won gold medals at the Olympics in 1996 and 2000. My time with TEAM USA is priceless to me. The sports experience, in combination with the fun and good friends, was worth every second of hard work that was put into my game.

The proudest moment of my athletic career was when the 1996 team was awarded the gold medal and my father was there with a picture of my mother who had passed away. This experience greatly eased the pain from college and also gave my father the knowledge that he and his wife had done a very good job of raising me and all their children.

When there is a failure for me, it haunts me. I have to get another opportunity and keep going, seeking restoration, trying to find what will heal the pain. Failure is what fuels the fire to keep going and never give up. This is one reason failure is positive; it is a motivator. I am so happy I kept going.

I was also very fortunate to be able to play professional basketball overseas. I played in Sweden, Hungary, Italy, and Turkey for seven years. I felt so blessed to have been able to earn a living while doing what I love.

During the early '90s, a women's professional league started in the USA. It failed within a couple of seasons. The WNBA was established in 1997. I was chosen to play for the Sacramento Monarchs that year. As of 2010, the league will begin its fourteenth year. I played eight seasons with the Monarchs. It was really special to play professional ball in the United States. Even though the team won the 2005 championship, the year after I retired, I felt I got to be a part of building toward that. It was great to be there and see it happen. I was honored when my number 6 was retired at ARCO Arena that year.

Playing professionally and being on Team USA was great because there was only one job, and that job was basketball. Playing at this level does involve a lot more than just team practice and games. A player who wants to really succeed must put in many hours outside of practice to truly reach full potential. For example, extra work may include weight lifting; private lessons to help with things like shooting form, footwork, and special shots; extra running; and lots of extra free throw shooting. Spending time stretching before and after practices and visualizing perfect basketball plays and shots are also an assist to reach full potential. At high levels, the mental game becomes a strong factor of success. A healthy diet is very important, and I was fortunate to learn about that while growing up.

Playing in the USA for eight seasons was really the icing on the cake for my basketball journey. I had a great experience with the Sacramento Monarchs, and I made lifetime friends. It was awesome to do what I loved to do for a living and have all the time I needed to completely focus on my career.

I did have one setback during those years. I suffered an ACL injury. This is a major ligament tear in the knee. This is a very common injury for basketball players, and this is why it is important to keep the knees strong. I was very fit, but unfortunately, the wrong twist at the wrong time can still cause this injury. The rehab took about one full year. It was a slow and tedious process to go through. It was worth the hard work as I was able to come back and play with the Monarchs and overseas.

It was very sad news during 2009 when the Monarchs' owners announced they were selling the team. No one bought the team, and the Monarchs were dispersed all over the WNBA. It was a tough emotional blow to see one of the eight original WNBA teams fold. It was a very sad time for all the players and the faithful Monarchs fans that we all appreciated so much. I was still working for the Monarchs then and had to find a new path to take also.

I am very proud to say that I was a first lieutenant in the United States Army. I served for four years. During that time, I was burning the candle at both ends, combining basketball, college, and serving my country. Scheduling time was a huge part of making it through. I wouldn't trade any of my experiences. I strongly believe that hard work pays. I really loved every moment.

As of 2010, I am currently retired from basketball. I now have a wonderful new daughter, Hope. I am thrilled to have her, and she keeps me very busy. I have coached some college basketball, and I am involved with local high school basketball by teaching and mentoring individuals and teams. I give private lessons, and I am very busy with motivational speaking engagements and basketball clinics.

During 2010, I had the honor of being inducted to the WNBA National Hall of Fame. This was really a thrill for me. I really have to say, it is tough to put into words how this honor made me feel.

I am looking forward to watching my daughter grow, staying involved with basketball in every aspect that I can, and helping others to reach their goals and dreams. The ability to teach and help others at something they love to do is priceless. I am fortunate to have the joy of my daughter and be able to teach the youth about something that I love—basketball and competition.

If I were to sum up the main reasons for my successful basketball journey, I would say this: I was fortunate to be raised in a very positive environment and to be a part of such a loving family led by two great parents. I learned to work hard and enjoy my journey at the same time. I believe that always remaining thankful and humble helped me to deal with success and failure well. The ability to deal with failure and disappointment and the never-give-up attitude was a big factor in continuing to be successful.

YOU WOULD BE AMAZED AT THE POWER WITHIN BY KEEPING
A GOOD ATTITUDE AND HAVING A PURPOSE.

It has been my pleasure to share this story for AN ATHLETE'S PERSPECTIVE, and I really hope my story can help you in your quest to reach your highest potential and to LIVE YOUR DREAMS.

ENJOY YOUR JOURNEY,

RUTHIE BOLTON

Richard Battles just before beginning his half triatholon after 18 months of hard work.

Richard out of the water after completing Stage 1, the 1.2 mile swim and looking good.

RICHARD'S STORY

It was a cold and stormy night . . .

I have been riding motorcycles since 1962, over forty-seven years now.

My wife, Kathy, and I created and sold motorcycle soft luggage. We have shared this business together for over thirty years. WE LOVE TO RIDE. We started doing track days together. These are events where you bring your own motorcycle, tape up the lights, and go out on the track for fun with other riders. There are A, B, and C groups for different levels and fun for everyone. It's not racing.

In 1999, a few of my friends and customers told me I should take my newfound skills to the track and actually RACE with the AFM local motorcycle club. At fifty-four years old, I decided to give it a try. It was all for fun anyway, right?

I club raced for four years and had a blast. The issue was my motorcycle weighed in at about 300 pounds, and I weighed in at over 220 pounds! The poor little machine only had 27 horsepower. I am 5'10" and should weigh about 175 pounds.

In the last couple of years of my racing career, I got turned on to bicycles by one of my race buddies' father and a customer who happened to be a rather good bicycle time trials expert.

On February 28, 2003, Kathy and I went down to the local bicycle shop, and Albert helped me purchase a $550 mountain bike and $650 worth of gear. Just how does that work anyway? More for the gear than for the bike. Wow! We put it all in the van and went back to the shop where we worked. I rode it home that day—seven miles. It took me almost forty-five minutes, and I almost died! But KING OF THE MOUNTAIN!

I felt I had just done something better for myself than I had ever done before, and it felt good inside. I started keeping records of my rides right from the beginning. I hoped to lose 50 pounds and ride my motorcycle faster than ever.

I rode 247 miles the first month and averaged 12 mph. By the end of May '03, I was down to 193! I had lost 30 pounds in three months! Now that I look back on that, it's unbelievable.

In May of 2003, I purchased my very first adult road bike, which I still ride to this day, a 2003 specialized Allez steel frame, 18 speed. I started riding with the Santa Rosa Cycling Club, and at this time, I really started thinking about riding the bicycle more than racing the motorcycle.

Early in 2004, my friend and motorcycle race buddy started training for the Sonoma County Half Vineman, and on one of his training rides, I met Coach, my newfound friend Bill. Bill is seven years older than me and an ex-bicycle racer from the '70s, and he is such a great inspiration to me. We hit it off right away and started riding together. He would train me without me knowing it. One ride would be all in the big ring, some would be all about cadence, and sometimes the ride would consist of all about climbing. I was getting in better and better shape and felt better than I have in twenty-five years.

During July of 2004, we had a good friend and his buddy come out from Phoenix to participate in the Vineman. They stayed at our house, and we helped them with the transition from swim to bike by taking their swim gear back for them.

As we were standing at the transition, watching the swimmers move to their bikes and pedal up the drive to the start of a 56-mile bicycle ride and then a 13.2-mile run, I made the big mistake of looking at Kathy and saying "I could do this."

I am not sure when I tried to register for the Half Vineman. I was sure I would not get in as it always overfills, but somehow, I got in. I received my paperwork and a beautiful Vineman bicycle jersey! I could not believe they sent me a jersey before the event! I gave it to Kathy and told her to hide it somewhere! If I did not finish the race, it was going to be burned and never worn on my back!

I purchased a Mario Cipollini replica aluminum-framed race bike and started pedaling harder than ever before. My rides were starting to average well over 18 mph, including rides with climbing involved.

On September 28, 2004, I jumped in the pool and floundered 250 yards. On October 4, 2004, I walked 2 miles, which took me thirty-five minutes.

I was OFF and RUNNING so to speak.

By the end of December of 2004, I was struggling with my weight STILL at 190 pounds. The Cipollini 16-spoke bicycle I was riding had a 185-pound limit on it! I was also having problems with cramping during my runs, which were not that long yet. I am sure I was burning five thousand calories a day and eating six thousand.

By February 4, 2005, I was at 185 and never looked back for the next five months!

The part that hurt worst was I lost my coach Bill. All of a sudden, we stopped riding together. I finally called him and asked what was up. He simply said, "When you're done with this dream of yours, call me and we'll ride again." It was not that he did not want to support me; it was that he was finished with racing and enjoyed riding his bicycle just for that and that alone.

I really needed a coach who knew about this sort of thing. I hired Vince. He was a forty-something Tri-Dog that kicked butt! He did not want the job, but I finally talked him into it.

I had issues with open water swimming. I could swim all day in the pool but panicked in the open water of the lake. I did a couple of Tri-for-Funs short training events in open water. I got a fifth-place trophy in one even though I was scared swimming in the open water. I worked through this fear by remembering the big race in the Russian River is never more than five- or six-feet deep.

In July, the month of the event, I was in the low 170s and I felt great! I touched 173 days before and after the event. I had lost the 50 pounds I had hoped to lose!

The event was the hardest single thing I have ever done in my life! The training for it was really hard. I documented it on our business website so people could see how I was doing. With everyone looking, I could NOT stop. The business website is RKA Motorcycle Soft Luggage.

This is a month-by-month chart from October of 2004 to July of 2005:

		Swim Yards	Bike Miles	Run Miles
Oct	'04	6,700	384	15.50
Nov	'04	7,500	325	34.50
Dec	'04	12,350	237	38.00
Jan	'05	19,200	295	25.50
Feb	'05	14,650	265	49.50
Mar	'05	14,950	425	82.50
Apr	'05	8,900	385	26.75
May	'05	8,400	400	58.50
June	'05	13,000	509	90.00
July	'05	15,900	231	60.00
Totals		121,550	3,456	480.75

This is an example of a typical week of training:

	Swim Yards	Bike Miles	Run Miles
Monday	1,000	11	4
Tuesday	1,500	32	0
Wednesday	0	0	7
Thursday	2,000	31	0
Friday	0	0	6
Saturday	0	60	0
Sunday	0	0	13
Totals	4,500	134	30

If not for my wife, Kathy, who fed me correctly and TOTALLY supported me, I could not have begun to do this.

So how did it go? Understanding I was a geek, solo clarinet player, and drum major in my high school band, sang in the choir, majored in art, never did anything athletically (except some swimming), and was fifty-eight years old, fat, and lazy only nine months before this event . . .

the official records show I
finished twelfth in my age group, 55-59,

swam 1.2 miles in 39.24 minutes,

bicycled 56 miles in 2:53:13 (at 19.2 mph),

and ran 13.2 miles in 2:34:36.

Running across that finish line was such an emotional moment. There has been nothing in my life I can compare this experience to.

I have continued to ride my bicycle with my wife, Kathy, and my friends, including Bill the coach. I still go to the gym, work out, and run. I really enjoyed the journey, and I say

GET A LIFE,

GET FIT,

STAY FIT.

RICHARD BATTLES

Richard on his bike during stage 2 the 56 mile bike ride and still looking strong.

Richard is crossing the finish line after completing stage 3 the 13.2 mile run.
He has just achieved a huge goal.
This is the great feeling that comes with hard work, dedication and using much or all of
The information that you have just read about.
AWESOME and PERFECT!

CONCLUSION

There are many things that go with building success. Much of it has been covered in the guide.

For the athlete who has read this, reaching for ways to improve, this information should help you greatly. I swear by it as I have lived it, experienced it all, worked, and still live my life the same way. Planning and preparation take care of many problems and really help making every day become a success. Living life with high self-esteem feels really good. Being honest, living with integrity, NEVER CHEATING, and GIVING YOUR BEST is the BEST!

"In a Nutshell," DESIRE, HARD WORK, SELF-RESPONSIBILITY, PERSEVERANCE, DETERMINATION, LEARNING, READING, FOCUSING, ATTITUDE, LOVE, CARE, INTENSITY, PRACTICE, PLANNING, PREPARATION, AND GIVING THINGS YOUR BEST is mostly what it is all about.

I can sleep at night because I always give my best at work when I am coaching and teaching, when I am mowing the lawn, or whatever the task may be. I run my life and my students with HONESTY, LOVE, CARE, HONOR, PRIDE, SELF-ESTEEM BUILDING, ENTHUSIASM, RESPECT, POSITIVE MESSAGES, and more. So far, the girls I have coached leave with much more confidence than they came to me with. They show me improvement game after game. They show me their heart. The results using these methods are completely amazing to me.

I've wanted to share this information for a long time now. I believe it will help young people and athletes to be more successful, to learn and improve at a much quicker rate, to have less frustration and more fun.

My dream and hope is, this information helps you in your endeavors and in life. This information is really my brain in a book. My dream is that everyone can endure the ups and downs of competition and life as smoothly as possible while enjoying their journey.

You should be able to ALWAYS ENJOY YOUR JOURNEY.

HIGHLY RECOMMENDED BOOKS AND MOVIES

Movies

Pay It Forward

Remember the Titans

Hurricane

We Are Marshall

Mr. Holland's Opus

Million Dollar Baby

Akeelah and the Bee

Coach Carter

Hoosiers

Rudy

Finding Forrester

Take the Lead

Books

The Inner Game of Tennis by Timothy Gallwey

The Power of Your Subconscious Mind by Dr. Joseph Murphy

ACKNOWLEDGMENTS

Bonnie, my life partner, and Roxy Brown, our Labrador retriever.
If our existence ended, I would want to be with these two souls at that time. That
is the best way I know how to express the way I feel about them.
It is much more than love.
Roxy passed on October 1, 2010.
We will meet her at the BRIDGE in heaven.
Now we have Jazzmin,
our blue Great Dane, and Skylar, our mantle Great Dane.
Our love for them is awesome.

My best friend, Mom, thank you for raising me with morals, teaching me to respect
all people. Thank you for letting me be the "tomboy" that I was in the '60s
and letting me be me, an extremely important gift for me.
No one could have a better mom than you.

My Aunt Patt, God rest her soul. I miss her. Thank you
very much for telling me the hard truth when I was so young. You saved me
so much time in learning about how what happened to me negatively affected me.
Thank you for connecting me with Pauline.

My grandmother, Margaret Jones, God rest her soul. I miss her.
My grandmother was the strong foundation of my entire family.

Larry Mathews, God rest his soul.
His wife, Barbara, and son, Butch.
Thank you for making me a professional, a "player," and a much
better person.

Larry, thank you for teaching me almost everything that is in this book. The main purpose of this book is to pass on your priceless lessons.

Pauline Pearlman, God rest her soul. Thank you for being my MFCC and one of my very best friends. You helped me so much to figure out who I am and to become who I am. You taught me how to let the negative things that happened to me not ruin my life. You taught me how to trust my gut and control emotions. You gave me the strength and knowledge to let out the kid in me as an adult, so I got to have fun. My childhood was no fun at all.

Howie Harris, Pauline's past husband, thank you for being a great MFCC and a great family friend. Thank you for making my mom happy.

Caren Franci, thank you for coaching basketball at SRJC, being a teacher, friend, mom, mentor, and more. Thank you for teaching me well. That knowledge enabled me to coach young girls at basketball twenty years later. Playing for you and teaching and coaching the girls have been two of the very best times of my life.

Donna Bender, thank you for strongly encouraging me to write this book. Thank you for all your hard work and suggestions for it.

The professional bowlers who embraced me, Tish Johnson, Dede Davidson, Virgina Norton, Cheryl Daniels, and Donna Hazel, thank you so much for all the support you gave to a weekend warrior attempting to compete with national touring professionals. Your friendship is appreciated.

Thank God for getting me to coaching youth basketball. This has been the most rewarding experience of all my athletic experiences. Thank you to my basketball players and parents. I can only hope that I taught you as much as I learned from all of you. The time that I spent with every single one of my players is the most priceless time that I have spent in my life. I love you all.

Arthur Dakesian, my sixth grade teacher. Art was a teacher who made me feel like someone. We played chess together at lunchtime. That was very special to me. He taught his students about much more than just the ABCs of school. He will always hold a special place in my heart.

Thank you for your great stories.
These are two people who are on my list of sports heroes:

Ruthie Bolton
and
Richard Battles.

From left to right Damond Edwards, Jared Waters and Ruthie Bolton with author Shirley Battles at front. Shirley gives a big thank you to these three great athletes for taking the time to be a part of this book.

Introducing Book 2

AN ATHLETE'S PERSPECTIVE

ON

YOUTH COACHING

A GUIDE TO POSITIVE COACHING,
MENTORING, AND
TEACHING LIFE THROUGH SPORTS

Teaching children about how to become successful, feel confident,
and reach their highest potential is a must for our world.

75% of children quit because they are not having fun.
When they quit, they go somewhere else,
and that may not be a positive environment.

This is a guide for youth coaches to assist them in learning how
to put winning aside and make every individual a winner.

Any athlete or young person will benefit from this information.

IT IS IMPERATIVE
TO MAKE YOUTH SPORTS A POSITIVE EXPERIENCE FOR OUR YOUTH.

SHIRLEY BATTLES
a professional athlete and volunteer youth coach/teacher

Inspirational stories are included,
written by successful athletes.

One story is by
RUTHIE BOLTON,
two-time Olympic gold medalist.

TABLE OF CONTENTS

FOREWORD

INTRODUCTION

IN A NUTSHELL

MENTORING

KEY PHRASES

KEYS

EXPANSION OF KEYS

PRACTICE GUIDELINES

VOLUNTEERING AND AGREEMENTS

STUDENT GUIDELINES

TEACHING QUESTIONS

CONCLUSION

STORIES FROM ATHLETES

ACKNOWLEDGMENTS

RECOMMENDED BOOKS AND MOVIES

INTRODUCTION

Coaching children at a sport may be one of the most important things you can do. Keeping children involved in a positive group of any kind is critical to all our futures. It is a fact that abused, unloved, and unattended children are 100% of the children and teens in our juvenile halls.

As adults, we must keep our children involved in positive extracurricular activities. There is a whole life outside of school. Fun and positive activities are what we all need our children to be involved in. Extracurricular activities are often the motivation for a child to do well in school. Children and teens involved with positive activities have a much better chance of staying out of trouble and staying on the straighter and narrower path of life.

There are a few things that are extremely important about youth coaching. The first one is that children must be having fun. A statistical fact is that 75% of children quit by age twelve because they are not having fun. This is a very sad statistic. When a child quits something positive, they may just start something negative. Having fun is a great reason for a child to stay involved.

Another important factor is to involve every player on your team. Treat every player as a person with respect. The goal is not to win but to create high self-esteem and make every child feel like a winner. One goal, as a youth coach, is to make every member of the team end the season feeling like he or she learned how to get better at something and go away with more self-confidence. If your weakest player has fun and leaves with more confidence, likely all your players did, and you have accomplished your goal. The win/loss record does not matter.

One way to accomplish this is to teach the team that each player always has a role. Every role is an important part of the team. Each player will know what their role is, and it is each player's goal to give their best at their role. Let the team know that if each player gives their best at practice and games, they are automatically winners. Giving your best is winning. Learning from any mistakes or failures will teach us what we need to get better at. Mistakes and failure will always exist so we will make the best of it and learn to embrace failure as our best teacher.

Youth coaching can be one of the most priceless times of your life. Creating a positive environment for the children to have fun and learn in is extremely rewarding. It is up to the adults to create a positive path for all our children to follow. We all need to do our part to make this planet a better place.

The goal in getting this information out is to assist youth coaches to do a great and fulfilling job at coaching and teaching our youth. Included are many tips on how to help you make the team run smoothly, accomplish goals, and have very few—if any—problems with parents and students.

Thank you for beginning to read about how to assist our youth in living positive and productive lives while having fun and enjoying a journey. Children are our future.